When Trump Changed

The Feminist Science Fiction Justice League
Quashes the Orange Outrage Pussy Grabber

Also By Marleen S. Barr

Scholarly Books:

Genre Fission: A New Discourse Practice for Cultural Studies
Lost in Space: Probing Feminist Science Fiction and Beyond
Feminist Fabulation: Space/Postmodern Fiction
Alien to Femininity: Speculative Fiction and Feminist Theory

Edited Scholarly Books:

Reading Science Fiction (co-edited with James Gunn and Matthew Candelaria)
Afro-Future Females: Black Writers Chart Science Fiction's Newest New-Wave Trajectory
Envisioning the Future: Science Fiction and the Next Millennium
Future Females, The Next Generation: New Voices and Velocities In Feminist Science Fiction Criticism
Women and Utopia: Critical Interpretations (co-edited with Nicholas Smith)
The Reader's Guide To Suzy McKee Charnas, Octavia Butler And Joan D. Vinge (co-edited with Ruth Salvaggio and Richard Law)
Discontented Discourses: Feminism/Textual Intervention/Psychoanalysis (co-edited with Richard Feldstein)
Future Females: A Critical Anthology

Novels:

Oy Feminist Planets: A Fake Memoir
Oy Pioneer!: A Novel

When Trump Changed

The Feminist Science Fiction Justice League
Quashes the Orange Outrage Pussy Grabber

Marleen S. Barr

Cover Design By
Maria Chavez

Edited By
Bob Brown

B-Cubed Press
Kiona, WA

Copyright

For my dear friend Nanette Schorr

'He told me that he wanted the [Wollman] skating rink named after him,' Mr. Koch recalled. 'I was thinking to myself, what arrogance. First the convention center and now the skating rink. I'm surprised he doesn't want Central Park renamed for him.'

The mayor suggested that the rink be renamed if Mr. Trump waived his $3 million bill to the city. Mr. Koch said Mr. Trump declined, but promised a generous gift in the future. 'I said no,' Mr. Koch wrote,' intimating I knew, with him, a promise for the future was worthless.' - Sam Roberts ["Ed Koch's Epic Feud with Trump Survives the Mayor's Death," *New York Times*, February 27, 2017]

'I just thought the only weapon I've really got is comedy. And if I can make this guy [Hitler] ludicrous, if I can make you laugh at him, then it's a victory of sorts. You can't get on a soapbox with these orators, because they're very good at convincing the masses that they're right. But if you can make them look ridiculous, you can win over the people. I think that was the thrust of it.' - Mel Brooks [Stephen Deusner, "Mel Brooks: 'The Only Weapon I've Got Is Comedy,'" *salon.com*, November 14, 2012, https://www.salon.com/2012/11/14/mel_brooks_th e_only_weapon_ive_got_is_comedy/]

A Note about Protagonist Professor Sondra Lear

Professor Sondra Lear, like Professor Marleen S. Barr, is a feminist science fiction scholar. Since Sondra appears throughout this collection, it would be helpful for readers to become acquainted with her.

Barr says that "Sondra is me—except for the fact that she's always in her thirties and she's thinner than I am now. Sondra has powers and abilities that are far beyond those of Marleen S. Barr. I created her as a power fantasy" [Marleen S. Barr, "If #MeToo Came True: Author Marleen S. Barr and K-B Have A Chat," *Excuse Me, I'm Writing*, March 8, 2018, http://www.kbgressitt.com/2018/03/08/from-k-b-and-friends/metoo-feminist-science-fiction-marleen-barr/].

According to *Foreword Reviews*, "Not everyone can be a feminist professorial pioneer involved with science fiction," proclaims the protagonist [of Barr's novel *Oy Pioneer!*], Dr. Sondra Lear, in this otherworldly satire. Whether on a Fulbright scholarship in Europe or seemingly the only Jewish feminist in Virginia, Sondra blazes her way through life in true pioneer fashion. She is an academic, a post-modernist, a lecturing feminist theorist, a science fiction critic, and a constant matrimonial disappointment to her mother" ["Oy Pioneer," *Foreword Reviews*, February 2004, https://www.forewordreviews.com/reviews/oy-pioneer/].

Barr's fellow Science Fiction Research Association Pilgrim Award winner for lifetime achievement in science fiction scholarship, Eric S. Rabkin, when writing to Barr, commented that the "boundary crossing [in Barr's novel *Oy Feminist Planets: A Fake Memoir*] seems to me the overarching theme, be it between Sondra and Marleen, reality and fiction, memory and imagination . . . or human and alien. . . . There is an indomitable questing, both of the imagination of the author and of the protagonist. . . . No one can be Sondra Lear (although you come close), but everyone can resonate with her joy in a continuing sense of future" [Eric S. Rabkin, Email to Marleen S. Barr, May 31, 2015].

Table of Contents

Foreword

Comedy often masks tragedy. In Marleen S. Barr's hilarious *When Trump Changed: The Feminist Science Fiction Justice League Quashes the Orange Outrage Pussy Grabber*, outrage underscores the tragedy of a good country having a bad leader.

Barr's stories presents situations in which a native New Yorker, feminist science fiction professor Sondra Lear, and alien (really alien) feminists take the president of the United States to task for being—well, who he is—and saying and doing the toxic, not to mention ridiculous, things that he does, against women, immigrants, the environment, world peace, and a basic sense of justice (or just basic sense).The stories, which address issues ranging from the presidential election to Trump's close encounter with Kim Jong-un, are replete with feminist extraterrestrials' spaceships landing on the While House lawn with traffic jam level frequency, a plethora of references to pussy grabbing, and blasts from the past (such as Bella Abzug, Cleopatra, and T. S. Eliot) who literally drop in to help make it possible for Trump to blast off and land in locales far far away from us.

Barr often parodies well-known stories to emphasize that Trump is most deliberately and strenuously an outrageous anti-Obama. Her scenarios are broad and outlandish, which fits her subject matter perfectly as she lampoons a broadly outlandish figure. But behind each encounter in which Sondra and her alien cronies who hail from feminist planets called by various uniquely feminine names (my favorite is Fallopia whose denizens are, of course, Fallopians), is an unspoken prefix: "If only I were in charge, this is what would happen!"

I could not agree with Barr more, not only as a feminist

but as an American, and a veteran (who does not respect a president who describes himself to troops as being "financially brave," especially since he pats himself on the back for the chances he takes with other peoples' money).

If Barr's science fiction scenarios came true, the current squatter in the White House would be evicted. Since the title Barr chose for her anthology alludes to Joanna Russ's "When It Changed" and she frames her stories with Mel Brooks' comments about the power of comedy, it is reasonable to assume that Barr wishfully hopes that parody—the impact of the Feminist Science Fiction Justice League—can make it so.

"Social integrity blossoms when feminist science fiction power fantasies for women become real," writes Barr at the conclusion of her story "Into the Chappaqua Woods."

Elizabeth Ann Scarborough,

2018

Trump and the Extraterrestrials

or

A Resounding Cosmic Political Chirp

It gave me great pleasure to read . . . 'With Faint Chirp, Scientists Prove Einstein Correct,' in which Albert Einstein and his 1,000 contemporary co-conspirators usurped that coveted position away from the presidential candidates. . . . At least for one day our pitiable earthly problems had to yield to the monumental collisions of higher powers. - Benjamin Bederson, "A Chirp That Affirms Einstein, and Thrills Us," *New York Times*, February 13, 2016, A3

Overload Arthur, a big giant head and chair of the United Planets Admissions Committee, began his address on behalf of Earth.

"My fellow Overloads, Earth's childhood has ended. Earthlings surely deserve to avail themselves of United Planets membership perks. Yes, I realize that Adult Swim is a very exclusive health club. But it is time to acknowledge that Earthlings are civilized enough to swim with us."

Overload Clarke, also a big giant head, stood up to voice his opposition. "What if we don't like Earthlings? We could be stuck with them. I go to Adult Swim to burn calories to shrink my big giant head. I don't want to fraternize with immature members."

"According to the United Planets Constitution, it is my right to nominate new civilizations," said Overload Arthur. "I will compromise, however." Had he not been a big giant head, he might have snapped fingers. "I propose a test."

"And what would such a test be?" asked Overload Clarke as he lifted a single eyebrow.

"I have sufficient faith in Earthlings to let them hear the chirping sound of two colliding black holes," Overload Arthur answered. "Give them their first evidence of gravitational waves. If they respond maturely, then they are in. If not, I defer to Overload Clarke." Big giant heads nodded at the wisdom of his words. "There was an Earthling named Einstein who, over a century ago, predicted ripples in the fabric of space/time. Even if he was an Earthling, Einstein was no infantile dummy. So too for contemporary humanity," concluded Overload Arthur.

Overload Arthur's compromise received unanimous support. Earth's scientists were permitted to hear the cosmic chirp. In the United States, the scientific discovery dominated the news cycle for an entire day.

Overload Clarke was not satisfied. "What difference does a day make?" he asked. "A one day hiatus from sandbox politics does not signify advanced civilization comportment. Arthur, my faction will obstruct your nomination." Multiple big giant heads nodded vigorously.

Overload Arthur's big giant head exploded in response. After he pulled himself together, he presented yet another compromise. "There's one way out of this stalemate. We use our heads and directly engage the Earthlings. America's Republican presidential candidates are the most childish humans on Earth. A Republican debate is going on as we speak. Let's beam down and establish first contact. If the candidates act like adults, then Earth will be admitted to the United Planets."

"I accept," said Overload Clark, whose big giant head did not explode.

Overloads Arthur and Clarke materialized in the debate auditorium just as Donald Trump was calling Ted Cruz a pussy.

"This portends well," said Overload Arthur. "'Pussy' means 'cute cat.'" Nothing childish here. Earthlings can successfully take their seat as United Planets members."

Trump looked up and saw two big giant heads hovering above the candidates. "Look at this," he said. "Now we have to contend with big giant heads. They're huge. But my head is bigger. These things are aliens. They're worse than Mexicans. They're rapists. No, hold that. These huge heads lack penises; they can't be rapists, the putzes. But we can build a wall to keep them out. I've made deals with aliens. I love the aliens. What do you aliens want?"

Overload Arthur answered Trump directly. "I want Earth to join the United Planets."

"And what's in it for us?" Trump asked.

"There are all kinds of perks. Earthlings would be eligible to join our posh health club Adult Swim, for instance."

"Now ya talkin'. Health clubs mean real estate development. But I have enough business on this planet. Why don't you involve Marco Rubio, take him out of my hair? When I spoke in South Carolina, I explained that Rubio's profuse perspiration could make foreign relations difficult. As I said, 'when we get in with Putin, we need people that don't sweat. I thought he just came out of a swimming pool' [Adam Gabatt, "Donald Trump Leaves Supporters Cold As He Accuses Rubio of 'Excess Sweating," *The Guardian*, February 16, 2016]. Marco's your guy."

"Can I get in here?" injected Dr. Ben Carson. "I'm a brain surgeon. I'm the perfect candidate to take on disembodied extraterrestrial big giant heads."

"No me, me. This is a job for my brother and my mommy," said Jeb Bush. "I want my mommy."

"I rest my case," Overload Clarke smugly intoned to Overload Arthur, whose big giant head hung in resignation.

Just as Overload Arthur was about to give up arguing that Earthlings were mature and civilized, a third head appeared. It was human and had a shock of grey hair which was more outlandish than Trump's hair.

"It's Einstein," declared Trump. "Smart guy. But I'm smarter. I went to great schools."

Overload Arthur knew that the tide had turned in his favor. "Albert, I am an alien intelligence who respects you. I came to this debate to prove that potential Earthling leaders can represent their planet by acting like orderly grownups. How can this objective be accomplished?"

Einstein had the answer. "Use the chirp emanating from the colliding black holes as a debate prompt. At the sound of the chirp, all candidates will have to exhibit maturity and civility."

"Einstein is not to be believed. He was a scientist. Science is bunk. And Einstein was a—you know, a person who has New York values. The chirp is the voice of God. This interpretation is a sign of true conservatism," intoned Cruz.

Anxious to augment their conservative credentials, at the sound of the chirp, the candidates acted like grownups—with one orange haired exception.

"I cherish New York values. George Bush is responsible for the 9/11 terrorist attacks which showcased those values. Albert, do you want to work with the Trump Organization? We can use your head," said Trump. Einstein did not answer him.

The big giant heads returned to their United Planets committee room. After the motion to have Earth join the United Planets met with success, Overload Clarke, though often disagreeing with the decision, never regretted it so much as this time. He went to his favorite relaxation destination and saw the plaque that hung on the wall, a bright golden plaque: "The Trump Adult Swim Club," it read.

Trump Dreams of Jeannie

Trump was ensconced in his Fifth Avenue aerie contemplating his Cabinet appointments. All of the chotchkes in the penthouse were gold, with one exception. His germ phobia kicked in as he noticed a smudged oblong lamp adorned with a spout and a semi-circular handle. Because the lamp was made of bronze, not gold, Trump made a mental note to complain to his decorator. Trump, who was a tad nervous about being president-elect, rubbed the lamp to assuage his anxiety. Smoke suddenly poured from the spout and wafted over the French provincial furniture. A rotund brown skinned young man—who wore pantaloons, a billowing sleeved shirt covered by a vest, a small tasseled hat, and pointed shoes—stood in front of Trump. Trump noted that he was closely encountering a foreigner from a shithole country.

"Are you a gay rights demonstrator? How did you breach my huge security?" snarled Trump.

"I materialized," answered the man.

"Materializing is as much bunk as global warming."

"Since you choose not to believe in science, you should accept that penthouse entry accomplished via materializing is possible. Where I come from, we materialize all the time."

"I'm afraid to ask, but where do you come from? Are you a rapist or a drug dealer?"

"A different realm. To make a long story short, I'm a genie. Genies do not commit rape or deal drugs. The name's Aladdin."

"Aladdin, huh. You're a Muslim. Register immediately and prepare for deportation."

"Exactly how to you intend to accomplish deporting a genie?"

"I'm the president-elect of the United States. I can do whatever the hell I want."

Aladdin wiggled his middle finger. Trump and all the golden home furnishings began to float.

"Put me and my property down immediately," demanded Trump.

"You are not exactly svelte. Getting you up was hard. I will do as you ask if you agree to my terms."

"Which are?"

"The genie realm constitution mandates that you make three wishes and I grant them."

"What's with this wish thing? I never wish for anything. I always get exactly what I want. I'm a billionaire."

"You cannot lie to a genie. Doing so results in an insatiable urge to eat cheese burgers and gain an inordinate amount of weight. That warning aside, remember that what you obtain must conform to the confines of reality."

"Put me down and I'll do the wish thing."

When Trump and the furniture simultaneously landed with a thud, he made more noise than the sofa. He straightened his oversized suit and faced Aladdin.

"First wish time," said Aladdin. "Go for something unreal."

"I have to do this pesty Cabinet post filling task. I need someone more offensive than Stephen K. Bannon. I wish that I can make Genghis Khan secretary of state."

The smell of a yak in heat permeated the penthouse. A man clad in a head covering appropriate to Stephen Colbert's "Big Furry Hat" sketch materialized. "Genghis," said Trump while extending his hand. "I'm the president-elect of the United States. I'm making you secretary of state."

Aladdin used magic to make it possible for Trump and Genghis to schmooze.

"Huh? What palace is this? I am going to conquer you."

"Oops," said Trump. "Aladdin I want a do over. I made a mistake. Genghis Khan is probably related to Khizr Khan, the Gold Star parent who brandished the Constitution against me. The people who supported me won't like it if I appoint someone named Khan secretary of state."

"Do overs are not allowed. You wished for Genghis Khan. Now deal with him," ordered Aladdin.

The yak was nibbling at the house plants while Genghis brandished his sword and looked out of the window.

"I don't think that I am in Mongolia anymore," said Genghis.

"You're most certainly not in Mongolia. You work for me. Put that sword down and listen to my terms," ordered Trump.

"All I want is to rape and pillage," said Genghis dejectedly.

"You can accomplish that here. You just have to call it grabbing pussy and pulling off con games."

"I'm in," acquiesced Genghis.

Trump tweeted that Genghis Khan was the new secretary of state. Liberal New Yorkers tried to convince themselves that Genghis Khan was preferable to Rudy Giuliani. All the Democratic elected officials and *New York Times* columnists who held their noses and said that they were willing to give Trump a chance to succeed were having second thoughts. Genghis opened Trump's refrigerator, took an entire roast in hand, and began to chomp on it. Trump's neighbor called the super to complain about the yak odor permeating her multi-million dollar apartment; she thought that living with the smell was worse than coping with the new security measures.

"Time for your second wish," announced Aladdin.

"I'm on a roll. I wish that Jack the Ripper could be secretary of housing and urban development."

A sinister looking man wielding a knife and dragging a corpse did the by now familiar to Trump materialization thing. Aladdin kicked the corpse under the sofa and made the knife disappear.

"Welcome to New York. I'm president-elect Donald Trump. You will play an important role in my Cabinet."

"All I care about is ripping people apart."

"Yes, that's your job description. Only we call it ripping people off and slashing budgets. Republicans want you to rip and slash with impunity. Just do it with a pen, not a knife. Cutting remarks are also okay. I'm particularly good at those," stated Trump.

"Cutting is cutting. Sounds good," answered Jack the Ripper.

"Third wish," said Aladdin.

"I can't do better than Genghis and Jack," said Trump as the two new Cabinet members retired to bedrooms to get some rest.

"Well, there is always Hitler," suggested Aladdin.

"No, Hitler is too much—even for me. Why should I cause a racist ruckus with Adolph when I have already appointed Jeff Sessions to be attorney general? Swastikas are appearing all over. The alt-right guys vociferously said 'hail Trump' at their Washington conference. My daughter married a Jew and converted. She's so hot—too hot for ovens. I need her and her husband to carry on my business interests. What I no longer need is you. I've gotten what I wanted from you. I will do things my way. Even though I can't deport Muslim you, I can get you the hell out of my apartment. I wish that you would disappear."

Aladdin dematerialized in a smoke cloud accompanied by a space time continuum disturbance rumble which was only felt in Hawaii. The governor of Hawaii assured his constituents that they were not facing North Korea induced nuclear annihilation.

Relieved that nuclear war was not ensuing, Trump picked up an elongated bottle which was rounded at the bottom and removed the cork. Pink smoke appeared in the room. A woman who looked and dressed exactly like Barbara Eden playing the sexy genie in the 1960's sitcom *I Dream of Jeannie* materialized.

"I'm a baby boomer. I know you. Hello Barbara. Strange that you are not in your eighties. But stranger things have happened today. You're somehow still very attractive," said Trump.

Trump reached out to kiss the woman and grab her pussy. His hands and lips were greeted with a nonlethal electric shock."

"I am not Barbara."

"Shit. Not another genie. I just got rid of a genie."

"I am not a genie. I am an extraterrestrial, a denizen of a feminist separatist planet. I appeared to be Barbara Eden so that you would not have a heart attack when you saw me in my true purple skinned four headed form. The electric shock is part of aversion therapy for pussy grabbers. By the time we are finished with you, you will never grab another pussy again. My clones and I are very nasty women."

Many clones of the extraterrestrial who also looked like Barbara Eden playing Jeannie appeared in the room.

"Sisters, what should I do with this deplorable lying, male chauvinist pig?" asked the extraterrestrial.

"Lock him up. Lock him up," shouted the clones.

"As you wish," the extraterrestrial said.

Faster than a New York minute, Trump found himself inside the bottle ensconced in front of a huge television set broadcasting Alec Baldwin imitating him on *Saturday Night Live*.

"I am a benevolent feminist separatist planet inhabitant. You will stay inside the bottle watching Baldwin portray your mendacious and malicious idiocy until a Democratic is elected President. I suggest that you spend your time dreaming of grabbing Jeannie's pussy," said the extraterrestrial as she corked the bottle—firmly.

Two Trump Heads Are Better Than One?

Professor Sondra Lear could not ignore the persistent pain in her molar. And thus it came to pass that she found herself sitting in an oral surgeon's chair preparing to have her tooth extracted.

"Do you want me to put growth material in your gum which will facilitate implant insertion?" asked Dr. Doogie Horowitz. Sondra, who was scared as hell that she was about to be decapitated, nodded her head affirmatively.

When she returned for her post-operative check-up, she asked for details about what had been inserted in her mouth.

"Bone," Horowitz said.

"What kind of bone?"

"Bone from a cadaver."

"What if the cadaver wasn't Jewish? I might have potentially *goyishe* bone cells reproducing in my jaw."

Sondra went home and fell asleep. Upon awakening, she felt a weird sensation on her shoulder. She looked into a mirror and saw a second head attached to her body. The head was not a normal head. It had a small pursed mouth, steely eyes framed by white makeup, and a very strange orange comb over. She gasped in horror as she recognized the features. Although she had become inured to the ubiquitous presence of the head on the television, having Trump's head attached to her body right next to her own head was the limit. Sondra immediately phoned the dental surgeon.

"I have an emergency. The cells in my teeth grew into Trump's head, not a new jaw bone."

"Oops," said Horowitz. "The cells I used came from Trump's deceased parents who were buried locally in New Hyde Park. Instead of simply generating new jaw bone cells, these cells grew into a completely formed Trump head."

"Will I gain weight? Trump is not thin and he eats, I can barely say it, fried taco shells. And if he has access to my hands does that mean that he can grab my pussy?"

"The Trump head has no control over your body."

"How do I get my normal Trump headless body back?"

"I need some time to research this question. It is an unprecedented situation."

Sondra decided to deal with the issue head on by seeking an audience with Trump himself in Trump Tower. She put on a burka to disguise the Trump head. Politically correct New Yorkers, loathe to stare at a burka-clad woman, would not notice the covered shoulder protrusion.

Sondra entered Trump Tower and asked to speak to Trump. Fearing that a woman wearing a burka had to be a terrorist, Secret Service agents swarmed around Sondra and frantically frisked her in search of a gun or a bomb. Instead they closely encountered Trump's head. It caused confusion.

"I'm not a terrorist," Sondra insisted. "I obviously have a huge problem."

"Huge," they all agreed while looking at the head.

"Trump has a swelled head. Maybe he has a suggestion."

The agents escorted Sondra to Trump's apartment. He became enraged when he saw his head attached to her shoulder.

"Get me a guillotine," screamed Trump. "Two Trump heads are absolutely not better than one."

"Sir, presidents are not allowed to behead people," said a Secret Service agent.

"Trump began to tweet: "Dr. Sondra Lear doesn't know how to use my head. Not." He then continued to shout. "I'll use the nuclear codes to explode the hell out of the imposter Trump head."

"Sir," implored the agent. "It is not advisable to deploy

nuclear weapons simply because the second Trump head hurts your ego."

"Can't we blame the Mexicans? I will initiate a travel ban to prevent any other Trump head from entering the country."

In response, Trump's alternative head harmlessly exploded. Dr. Horowitz closed the hole in Sondra's shoulder. She recovered completely.

Swansong for Trump

But Paul [Manafort, the former Trump Campaign Manager] didn't know how to play the Trumpet. - Maureen Dowd, "Open Letter From Mr. Trump," *New York Times*, August 21, 2016, 11

Donald J. Trump supporters sell T-shirts emblazoned with 'Trump That Bitch!' One reporter noted that mentions of Mrs. Clinton at a Trump rally in Greensboro, N.C., were greeted with gleeful shouts of the word ['bitch']. - Andi Zeisler, "The Bitch America Needs" *New York Times*, September 11, 2016, 2

Professor Sondra Lear decided that she could not—not for one more microsecond—abide Trump's diatribes. "I wish I could do something science fictional to silence Trump," she said aloud. She was distraught to the extent that she was talking to herself. "It's a shame that even though I know all of this science fiction theory, I can't reify my knowledge. I wish I could send Trump to the Phantom Zone. I wish I could give him a one-way ticket for a voyage to Arcturus—or to any planet located in a galaxy far, far away. Fantasy princesses have fairy god mothers. Oy, just because a feminist theorist really doesn't fit the usual Jewish American princess qualifications, why can't I have a fairy god mother? I wish I had a fairy god mother."

"Your wish is my command," said a patrician voice. Sondra's office was suddenly smoke filled. When the smoke cleared, Sondra saw a white-haired lady wearing tailored clothing and pearls.

"The late Mrs. Bush?" Sondra said incredulously. "Why have you materialized in my office? Are you a ghost?"

"I am your fairy god mother."

"My fairy god mother? I'm a fervent liberal Democrat. How can the quintessential Republican matriarch be my fairy god mother?"

"We are now on the same side, dear. My antipathy for Trump knows no bounds. The nerve of him calling my Jeb low energy. It was Jeb's turn. Besides, since you asked for a fairy god mother, your wish has been granted. I have come to tell you how to shut Trump's mouth."

"I'm listening."

"Use semantics."

"Even though I'm a literary critic, I don't see how words can silence Trump."

"People routinely play with the name 'Trump.' They mention 'trump cards' and being 'trumped.' But nobody applies 'trump' to animals. Donald Trump is for the birds; trumpeter swans can counter him."

"Trumpeter swans? I'm still listening."

"Yes, trumpeter swans. Hitchcock knew that birds have power. As a bona fide fairy god mother, I fraternize with fantastic creatures—such as fire breathing trumpeter swans. You can summon one and ride her to a destination of your choice."

"Like a cross between Uber and Dragon Riders?"

"Exactly. When riding astride a fire breathing trumpeter swan, you can look Trump straight in the eye and say, 'You're fired.'" I love illocutionary force. I'm in."

Mrs. Bush told Sondra that a fire breathing trumpeter swan flock was roosting in the university parking lot. The flock leader waddled toward Sondra, squawked a greeting, lowered her neck, and extended her wing. Sondra climbed up and clung to the swan's neck. Since sitting on the back of a giant swan is quite comfortable, Sondra remained calm.

Ready for takeoff, she recalled that Trump was scheduled to speak in Greensboro, North Carolina later that evening. "Fly to Greensboro," she said. The leader ascended as the flock lined up in formation behind her. Soon Sondra and her avian colleagues were hovering over the Trump rally.

Within minutes the swans had the red-hatted crowd cowed. They herded them into a parking lot next to giant pickup trucks and mid-80's Cadillacs.

"Everyone pile up your 'Make America Great Again' signs," ordered Sondra from her perch. When the giant fire breathing trumpeter swan leader opened her beak, even the burliest racists complied. Curses were heard as the crowd relinquished their placards. The swan directed a flame at the piled signs and, hence, burned them to smithereens.

"This swan must be a Hillary supporter," proclaimed Trump, who had caught a golf cart and ridden to the parking lot. "A crooked, lyin' fire breathing bird. Look at how huge it is. A rapist swan. An immigrant from a fairy tale. I'm going to build a wall."

"You can build all the walls you want," retorted Sondra. "There are more such swans where these came from. They can fly over your wall."

"I'll have the swans shot and turned into barbeque. Great marketing potential: Trump Trumpeter Swan Steaks."

The flock leader aimed a flame at Trump's red baseball cap. Just as his hair was about to catch fire, a Secret Service agent threw a bucket of water on his head. Regaining his composure, Trump said, "The second amendment advocates need to do something about these swans."

The entire flock squawked and drowned Trump out. They flew low over the crowd and set fire to all the "Make America Great Again" hats. The swans used magic fire which at once burned hats and left heads unscathed.

Flummoxed and flustered by the fire breathing flock's sound barrage, windbag Trump deflated into dumbfounded silence.

Barbara Bush materialized.

"You're fired," she trumpeted to Trump in tandem with Sondra.

Mrs. Bush snapped her fingers. A mirror appeared. "This is a mirror mirror on the wall," she said to Trump. "Who is the most ludicrous of us all? Until you can answer, you'll spend eternity in front of this mirror watching a replay of the election in which Hillary wins over and over again. By the way, her Inauguration Day crowd size will be bigger than yours."

Into the Chappaqua Woods

or

A Spaceship From A Feminist Separatist Planet Lands on Trump's White House Lawn

Clinton can't spend the rest of her days in hiding and on nature walks. The woods around Chappaqua, N.Y. are lovely, dark, and deep, but really. No one ever mistook her for a forest nymph. She's a creature of pavement, pantsuits, and politics. Shouldn't she get back to all three? - Frank Bruni, "Rumors of Hillary Clinton's Comeback," *New York Times,* January 8, 2017

Professor Sondra Lear was sobbing in her office. The inescapable fact that Trump was really the president of the United States devastated her. Although she had experienced the deaths of loved ones and illnesses, she felt that President Trump was not a typical vicissitude. Having your country's national character become gone with the wind during one election night is not normal. While walking to the subway on the morning after the election, Sondra felt like a participant in a funeral procession. Around her, the usual hurried insensitive New York throngs were ashen faced and dazed. Sondra, knowing that she could not survive living in Trump's racist and misogynist America, was primed to use all of her resources to cope.

As the wife of the metrosexual French Canadian art

historian Pepe Le Pew, if Sondra showed up at the Canadian border, the Canadians would have to let her in. "I want to move to Canada," Sondra announced to Pepe.

"*Non. Jamais.* I moved here thirty years ago and I am too old to go back and freeze my ass off."

"Because you're not American, you don't understand how I feel about Trump."

"Be that as it may, I refuse to return to Canada."

Seeing that going to Canada was a no go, Sondra focused on a new destination: Chappaqua. Lacking the clout to make an appointment to speak with Hillary, after hearing that Hillary was spotted walking in the Chappaqua woods, Sondra decided to use the woods as a viable Hillary meeting place. Even though urban Sondra did not "know from" woods, as an English professor, she was aware that the Shakespearean green world is a magical place which functions outside society's confines.

Sondra boarded Metro North, disembarked at the Chappaqua station, walked into the woods, and began to search for Hillary. She soon found a discarded lipstick and a white Ralph Lauren pantsuit jacket. Hot on the Hillary trail, Sondra knew that her quarry was in the vicinity. And then she saw *her.* Makeup-less Hillary—attired in a fleece, sweatpants, and sneakers—was standing in front of a large tree.

"Hello Secretary Clinton. I hope that I'm not disturbing you. I'm Professor Sondra Lear. Could I bother you with a quick question?" Since Sondra was a New Yorker, she didn't wait for an answer. "How can you cope with being so qualified to be president and losing your chance to a—I have no words to describe him."

Hillary pointed to a door embedded in the tree trunk. A sign on the door read "President Dummkopf Drumpf Escape Hatch." Hillary opened the door and beckoned toward Sondra to follow. A white rabbit carrying a copy of *The Female Eunuch* scampered in front of them. Sondra walked through the door and began slowly to fall down a hole. She passed shelves filled with cut up bras, nonfat dressing sodden salads, worn Birkenstocks, and pictures of Gloria Steinem, Bella Abzug, and Betty Friedan. Sondra landed with a thud next to Hillary. They were both standing near a tall authoritative woman wearing a gold jumpsuit and thigh high boots—and a small away team spaceship. Hillary and Sondra were located in an extraterrestrial garage.

"Don't panic," said the alien. "I am Zyra. I come from a feminist separatist planet. Our Motherboard Executive Council has been monitoring Earth with the intention of making first contact with feminist Earthlings. When Board members discerned that Trump was the president of the United States, their heads exploded. Really. Luckily, we can regenerate new heads. But that's another story. The Board instructed me to build a Trump resistance movement by engaging with appropriate American women. I chose Hillary and a feminist science fiction expert. I am a harmless feminist extraterrestrial envoy who wishes to counter Trump's adverse impact upon Earthling women."

"I'm perfectly calm," said Sondra. "I've spent my professional life studying feminist aliens and, hence, I am used to them. Zyra please don't feel badly that I am more excited about meeting Hillary than closely encountering you. Yes, finding myself in a spaceship launch pad located inside a tree is highly unusual—even for me. I love you, Hillary. What will become of us under Trump? I'm good with the tree hole, the spaceship, and the extraterrestrial. But I can't deal with a President Trump."

"I appreciate your concern. I think we should listen to Zyra," Hillary stated calmly.

"I am going to show you the future," Zyra said as one of the garage walls turned into a large viewing screen. Watch Trump's future State of the Union Address."

The on screen Trump was fatter and more haggard than the Inauguration Day Trump. He began to speak: "My fellow citizens of the United States of Trump. God bless America—and God, as you are aware, due to my new title, means me. I didn't get enough attention as a mere president. I had to live in the White House and follow all of those god damn rules and protocols; I especially hated those daily intelligence briefings. Luckily, after Putin made us kiss and make nice, Bannon figured out how to con you all into elevating me from mere president to God of the United States. It is great, really great, to have my picture on our money. And 'In Trump We Trust' is such an improvement. Very, very, much better. I did a deal to buy the Manhattan Olympic Tower Building from the Onassis Foundation, and I have renamed it Trump Mount Olympus Tower. Now, there have been some changes. For the better. You know that. As we are all aware, everyone except white Christians have been successfully removed from the homeland. It was tough to accomplish but ya gotta do what ya gotta do. There is still one big thing to do. And it's gonna be hard. I've been married three times, so I tell you I know how to do it. We're gonna have to get rid of all the ugly women. All the surviving women, the ones who rate a seven or higher, will be placed into one of two categories: Hills or Melons. The Hills, like Hillary, are smart women, but at least they are hot too. Now these women can never achieve the goals men achieve. No matter how hard—a word which does apply to me, I haven't mentioned me in the last five seconds—they try, they will face fruitless uphill battles. The Melons are named in honor of my fourth wife Melonia—my third wife Melania, who was too old to be a ten, was sacrificed and replaced with a twenty-one year old. The Melons, who have great rounded tits and asses, will do nothing but shop, perform sex acts, and give birth. Does this make the United States great again   for white men or what? No wonder you guys worship me. Our union is strong. And so my fellow Christian white males, ask not what your country can do for you. Ask what you can do for Trump. God, that is to say me, bless the United States   of Trump." The screen went blank against the audience's chants of "U.S.T., U.S.T" and "*Heil* Trump."

Trying to keep from fainting, Hillary and Sondra told Zyra that they would do anything to prevent this vision from becoming a real historical fact.

"Anything?" asked Zyra.

"Yes, anything," Hillary and Sondra said in unison.

"Would you enter a spaceship and go to another planet?"

"Absolutely."

Sondra chimed in to add a proviso: "On our way to the planet, can we please stop off to pick up my husband? He refused to go back to Canada because it's cold there. Is your planet cold?"

"Yes about the husband. My planet is s a tropical paradise replete with feminist theorists who write science fiction."

"Sounds like Sondra heaven. My husband likes to make me happy. He will be on board with boarding your spaceship," Sondra said.

"Ditto for Bill," Hillary added.

"Step into my shuttlecraft and fasten your seat belts," Zyra instructed.

Hillary and Sondra did as they were told. Zyra started her countdown: "Ten, nine, eight, seven."

"Wait. Stop the countdown," shouted Sondra. "I have a question. How are you going to get the shuttlecraft out of the tree?"

"Our matter alteration method is beyond your comprehension. Just trust me and think of it as a baby exiting a pussy."

"Maybe I have been an English professor for too long and Trump's edict that political correctness is punishable by death aside, I must say that 'vagina' is the more appropriate word—when no grabbing is involved," intoned Sondra.

"I never heard of 'vagina' perhaps because I have only been listening to Trump and his henchmen and they say 'pussy.' I will be sure to add 'vagina' to my vocabulary,' said Zyra.

Without further ado, the shuttlecraft flew upward, left the tree door in its wake, and landed on the White House lawn. Zyra opened the hatch, exited, walked toward a security guard and said "Take me to your leader."

A tall fat orange-haired man who could be described

by multitudinous unflattering adjectives appeared near the South Portico. "You're so smokin' hot. You're even hotter than Ivanka. If she weren't my daughter. . . . But you're not my daughter. Do you wanna be the next Melonia?" said Trump as he reached out to grab Zyra's pussy. Heat rays emanated from Zyra's eyes. Adjusting the temperature to cause sexual predator punishment pain rather than permanent damage, Zyra aimed the rays at Trump's left hand. Trump used his right hand to pull a gun from inside his oversized suit jacket. He aimed at Zyra's chest and fired. The bullet bounced off.

"Wow. Great tits," said Trump. "Such a shame that you're an alien, an immigrant. I'm deporting you. Go back to where you came from."

"You lack the power and ability to deport me to where I came from. I am a denizen of Kryptonia. The red sun in our sister solar system in relation to Krypton never exploded. All denizens of Kryptonia have super powers on Earth. I have more power in my little finger than you have in your entire military industrial complex. Imagine being attacked by an army of super powered women from a feminist separatist planet. And you had difficulty with Rosie O'Donnell and Megyn Kelly. On another subject, Professor Lear would say that like 'pussy,' 'tits' is an improper locution to emanate from a president's mouth. What is the proper word, Sondra?"

"I would say 'bosom' or 'breast,'" Sondra suggested.

"'Breast' sounds like it applies to chickens," mused Zyra.

"English is a difficult language. But your reference to poultry gives me an idea of what we can do with Trump. What I am suggesting applies to a more huge bird than a chicken. I'm talking turkey—as in presidential turkey pardon. Let's pardon Trump. When they go low, we go high," suggested Sondra.

"As you wish," said Zyra. "I will spare Trump's life— and bring about regime change immediately." Zyra snapped her fingers. A resounding rendition of "Hail to the Chief" permeated the White House lawn as Trump was whisked away to live out his days on a turkey farm in Kentucky. Hillary walked into the White House to assume her rightful place as president of the United States.

Hillary and Bill and Sondra and Pepe did take a trip on Zyra's spaceship. After President Hillary Clinton appointed Sondra to be ambassador to Kryptonia, the foursome journeyed their together. The Clintons attended Sondra's induction ceremony before returning to the White House. Sondra and Pepe enjoyed Kryptonia's tropical climate until they were called home upon the election of Hillary's successor President Elizabeth Warren.

The magical Chappaqua woods green world is a real alternative fact. Under the auspices of Presidents Clinton and Warren—leaders who believed climate change to be a true fact—the green world flourished. Social integrity blossoms when feminist science fiction power fantasies for women become real.

Duck, Donald: A Trump Exorcism

When Trump, near the end of his second term, sat on his golden Trump Tower toilet, he was in for a big surprise. After eliminating—and still ignoring the fact that the majority of Americans wished to eliminate him from office—he looked into the golden bowl. The toilet was filled with bright red liquid.

Feeling alarmed, Trump phoned Dr. Ben Carson to ask for a diagnosis. "Donald, I am a brain surgeon. I don't do rectums," Carson said. "And furthermore, I haven't practiced medicine in years. Since I am spending all my time using my experience as someone who has lived in houses to serve as Housing and Urban Development head, my medical ability has become a little rusty. Although you are not concerned with professional qualifications—everyone remembers how you hired a pollution lover to run the Environmental Protection Agency—I must say that I am not able to help you."

"What should I do?"

"Get a colonoscopy."

"Are there any ass doctors left?"

"I regret to remind you that most of the ousted Obama administration H.U.D. employees got jobs as doctors. It was logical for them to pull this switcheroo. They figured that if a doctor who lacked government agency experience could run H.U.D., then H.U.D administrators could be employed as doctors. Choose wisely in regard to the physician you allow to probe you. These people have memories. And frankly, sir, would you like to spend all day looking up assholes? Pussy grabbing is a lot more fun."

After Trump's symptoms continued and he was certain that he had colon cancer, he again sought Carson's advice. "You need to have surgery," Carson said.

"Are there any colon cancer surgeons left?"

"I am not sure. As you are aware, after you rescinded Obamacare, most people could not afford to see actual doctors. The whole medical system collapsed. Real doctors gave up their practices and were replaced by alternative doctors—such as the former H.U.D. folks. I will refer you to America's last qualified colon cancer surgeon."

Trump was wheeled into the operating room. The last of the Mohicans in relation to colon cancer surgery, Dr. Cochise Sitting Bull, slit open Trump's abdomen and peered inside. He saw, perched atop the president's bloated spleen, a bright red devil waving a trident. The devil's feet were resting firmly on a cancerous colon tumor. Afraid to remove the devil from inside Trump, the doctor left the devil where it was, extracted the cancer, rerouted the colon to an Ivanka designed colostomy bag, and sewed Trump up. Shocked by finding a devil within someone he considered to be a horror, Dr. Bull had a heart attack. Since cardiologists no longer existed, Bull died.

Trump did not enjoy life with an ostomy bag. Melania divorced him.

"I took all of your shit in order to have money beyond my wildest dreams. But that was alternative fact shit. I didn't sign up to deal with real shit," said Melania as she went down the Trump Tower escalator for the last time.

Trump could not cope with the ostomy bag hanging from his now flawed body. Alec Baldwin, comedic ally using Trump's condition against a background tape of Trump mimicking the handicapped *New York Times* reporter, participated in a *Saturday Night Live* skit involving a plastic bag filled with chocolate ice cream. Chocolate ice cream sales plummeted. Unable to endure further public humiliation, Trump chose to have reconstructive surgery. After again facing the lack of a qualified surgeon and reasoning that a rusty brain surgeon was better than a former H.U.D. employee, Trump convinced Carson to perform the surgery.

Bull never told Carson about the devil. The latter doctor had a great surprise in the operating room. "Enough already," said the devil as he jumped out of Trump and landed feet first on the operating room floor. "I wasn't alone in there," he continued as a plethora of gremlins, trolls, witches, and even a fire breathing dragon followed in his wake. Carson looked as if he had seen a ghost. "Don't be so surprised. Trump is not thin. He has a big abdomen. There was a lot of room for all of us," said the devil. And with a great grin he added, "But wait, there's more." He jabbed his trident into a particularly swollen portion of Trump's colon. It burst.

Flying feces joined the supernatural creatures parade. "Duck. Donald's shit is hitting the fan—again. Everyone take cover," Carson said to the operating room staff. Afterwards, when Carson supervised the sew up and cleanup, Trump opened his eyes in the recovery room. He saw a young attractive black nurse. (Unlike doctors, qualified nurses still existed.) "Since you're helping me, I can respond to you as a person," said Trump. "So even though you rate as a nine point two, I won't grab your pussy. Such a shame that you live in a crime ridden, drug infested, murder sodden ghetto."

The biopsy, done by secret agreement at a Canadian lab, told the story. Trump never had colon cancer. The red liquid in the toilet bowl was merely devil urine—a red shower. Even Putin could not have contrived this alternative fact. The surgery, which exorcised the evil living inside Trump, had not been a waste. No longer a loud mouthed narcissistic barbarian, Trump reinstated Obamacare and stopped substituting alternative facts for facts. When Elizabeth Warren followed him as president, Trump made sure that a smooth power transition ensued. In memory of Dr. Cochise Sitting Bull, Trump never again called Warren "Pocahontas."

During Warren's inauguration ceremony, Trump stood beaming next to the new Mrs. Trump. Mrs. Trump the fourth was seventy-five years old and she was not thin. Trump never found out that she was also not human. This spouse was a feminist separatist planet denizen sent to Earth to keep Trump in line—just in case he might have a relapse. To make Trump feel comfortable and to compensate for her lack of American popular culture knowledge, extraterrestrial Mrs. Trump presented herself in an Eastern European guise as the long lost clone of one Angela Merkel. Trump and "Hildegard" Trump lived happily ever after. He never made his alien wife register as an illegal immigrant.

Let Melania Eat Rugelach

Zephyr Zimmerman and Shoshanna Schwartz, neighbors who had been besties since their college days a decade earlier, were sunbathing on their Sutton Place apartment tower roof deck and sipping white wine spritzers. They applied sunscreen while admiring each other's chartreuse nail polish applied that morning at one of Manhattan's trendiest nail salons. It was Zephyr, always the more observant of the two, who noticed that the wind, instead of blowing across the deck as usual, was moving vertically. Then the women saw a strange vehicle touch down near them. Shoshanna, an avid science fiction movie fan, knew that she was closely encountering an extraterrestrial shuttlecraft.

A tall thin blonde woman wearing a gold jumpsuit and knee-length gold boots emerged from the hatch. The two Manhattanites immediately noticed that a wedding ring was absent from the alien's teal blue nail polished finger. With the confidence of *Legally Blonde* protagonist Elle Woods' client immediately recognizing that Elle was the best lawyer, the women instantaneously knew that they were meeting someone of their own ilk.

"Hi," Shoshanna calmly said to the alien. "Great nail polish. Would you like a spritzer?"

"I'm Nyra Nussbaum," the alien answered. "I hail from the feminist separatist planet Mikvah. Mikvahians spend a lot of time schvitzing and bathing on our hot watery world. After monitoring New York City, it is clear to us that you have a huge problem. More specifically, Mikvahians believe that Melania Trump is a terrible role model for Earth women."

"Absolutely," intoned Zephyr. "Thousands of New Yorkers have signed a petition to get Melania out of Trump Tower and into the White House where she belongs. Women like Shoshanna and I pay our own Manhattan tower dwelling place bills. I'm a fashion editor and she's a buyer for Bloomingdale's. We resent having our taxes go to protect Melania. Our privilege does not blind us to the fact that the tax money could be better spent helping our fellow New Yorkers."

"Great that we concur," said Nyra. "I landed on your roof deck because you are the perfect Earth women to help me solve the Melania moocher problem. I need your help because Mikvahians can only use our superior powers and abilities in conjunction with women who are native to the planets we meddle in."

"How can we help you?" asked Shoshanna and Zephyr in unison.

"You can accompany two of the most kickass Earthlings who ever lived, women who were the antithesis of Melania, to Trump Tower."

"Who do you have in mind?" Zephyr asked with excitement.

"Bella Abzug and Betty Friedan."

"I agree that Bella and Betty are not the same animal as Melania. But there is one problem," said Zephyr.

"Which is?"

"They're dead."

"Mikvahians can resurrect deceased feminist Earthlings. We give them real world agency as ghosts. Are you in?"

"Certainly."

Bella Abzug and Betty Friedan materialized on the roof deck.

"What has the world come to since my demise?" asked Friedan. "Melania epitomizes everything I railed against in *The Feminine Mystique*."

"She's the feminist mistake," shouted Abzug.

Shoshanna and Zephyr were impressed. "Even though Bella and Betty are not wearing chartreuse nail polish, we are good to go with them to Trump Tower," said Zephyr.

"Excellent," said Abzug.

Friedan leaned into consult with Abzug. They whispered, and two shopping bags materialized. "Come along ladies," Friedan said. "We have some things to pick up on the way."

Shortly, Shoshanna and Zephyr, accompanied by a very large hat and a copy of *The Feminine Mystique* floating in midair, as that was all that could be seen of Bella and Betty, walked along Fifth Avenue and made their way to the Trump Tower entrance. Shoppers at Saks Fifth Avenue were more disturbed that Bella's hat was out of style rather than appearing to move under its own reconnaissance.

Once at Trump Tower, the two young women waited outside while the hat and the book sailed past the very expensive Secret Service agents. The agents, after all, were not trained to deal with deceased celebrity New York feminists. They also clearly had never watched *Turner Classic Movies* and were completely oblivious to ghostly apparitions who function as ectoplasms similar to the ghosts depicted in the 1950's movie and television show *Topper*. While Abzug and Friedan did their invisibility thing, Zephyr and Shoshanna killed time shopping in Tiffany's.

The ghosts walked through Trump's apartment door. Once inside, they became visible, put their shopping bags on an imported marble countertop, and turned to confront Melania.

"Enough already with you using your body to garner riches. You are a disgrace to womanhood," said Abzug with her trademark directness. "Get the hell outta here and stop draining New York tax payers."

"Tax payers?" sneered Melania. "Let them eat cake." She then ordered her butler to throw cake slices out of her living room window. A pigeon flock closed in as the cake hit Fifth Avenue with a thud.

"You will be the one to eat cake," said Friedan. "Bella, it's time."

"Bella reached into her shopping bag and removed a tray of Entenmann's rugelach, and another, and another. But there was more: wrapped sandwiches, jumbo knishes, stuffed cabbage, and steaming soups. Soon the counter was covered.

The Trump's golden living room was filled with a huge variety of the most fattening food on Earth. Two dozen cheeseburgers rounded the collection out, perched precariously on the edge of the golden sink.

"If you don't leave Trump Tower immediately if not sooner, your only nutrition source will be Eastern European Jewish food," said Abzug, opening her own bag. Melania warily watched noodle pudding, matzo balls, stuffed derma, bagels schmeared with cream cheese, blintzes, hamantashen, challah, potato knishes, and kasha varnishkas made only with varnishkas join the rugelach. "You will get fat. You will lose the body which serves as your meal ticket."

"And how do you intend to imprison me in this multimillion dollar penthouse you have transformed into Zabar's?" asked Melania haughtily.

"We will build a wall," said Friedan. She gestured to the entry where Bella was already using copies of *The Feminine Mystique* as bricks. She had smeared them with hardened latke batter used as mortar.

Melania stubbornly remained imprisoned behind the feminist tome/latke innards-made wall for two weeks. Seeing that the knishes were causing her to gain weight in her kishkes, she panicked and lost her resolve. Shoshanna and Zephyr, wearing the diamond earrings they had bought in Tiffany's, cheered Abzug and Friedan on. Nyra applauded while seated in her shuttlecraft hovering outside Trump's bathroom window.

Melania told the ghosts that she was ready to surrender and leave Trump Tower. As Nyra prepared to help

Melania enter the shuttlecraft set to land on the White House lawn, the now noticeably bordering on zaftig Melania had a change of heart. "Hell no, I won't go," she shouted.

"Thousands of New Yorkers want ya out," screamed Abzug. "Let's start packing."

"I get the hint," said Melania. "I need an alternative to going to the White House. If I show up there fatter, Donald will throw me out on the street. I will be homeless on Pennsylvania Avenue. I have a better idea. I want to follow in the footsteps of South Korea's ousted female president Park Geun-hye. She is living in prison. I want to reside on Rikers Island. If I live in a high security prison, New Yorkers will pay much less to protect me. Becoming sexual prey in there can't be worse than having to service Donald. And, best of all, the food is terrible. I will lose weight. They don't serve rugelach in Rikers."

"Suit yourself," said Abzug.

That is exactly what Melania did. Immediately upon arrival at Rikers, she traded her little black Saks dress for an orange jumpsuit prison uniform. "Orange is the new black," said Zephyr, still in mourning after the election of the orange outrage president.

Shoshanna, Zephyr, Nyra, Bella, and Betty spent a final evening on the roof. Shoshanna and Zephyr invited their fellow Upper East Side resident Gloria Steinem over to have a reunion with Abzug and Friedan.

Melania, alone in her cell, ate bread and water with the hope of winning the war against her new cellulite.

Abzug and Friedan decided to haunt the White House. Trump, alone at night with his cheeseburgers and Abzug and Friedan's big mouths, went over the edge and soon was allowed to join Melania at Rikers. Melania begged Nyra for help. "Ivanka changed. Ivanka became Jewish. If Ivanka can be Jewish, then I can be an extraterrestrial feminist planet denizen. Nyra, please take me to your home planet Mikvah. Anything has to be better than living in a cell with Donald."

Nyra granted Melania's request. Melania lived happily ever after enjoying Mikvahian healthy cuisine: carrot *tzimmas*, lox, and defatted chicken soup.

Mike Pence developed a phobia over large hats.

Marleen S. Barr

'Just the Two of Us'

or

Trump Comes On to Comey

As I listened to James Comey . . . tell the Senate Intelligence Committee about his personal meetings and phone calls with President Trump, I was reminded of something: the experience of a woman being harassed by her powerful, predatory boss. There was precisely that sinister air of coercion. . . . Comey received a last-minute dinner invitation from the president and then learned it would be 'just the two of us'. . . . With the power of the presidency at his disposal, Mr. Trump thought that he could use the psychology of coercive seduction on the nation's chief law enforcement officer. - Nicole Serratore, "James Comey and the Predator in Chief," *New York Times*, January 9, 2017

At New York's Inner Circle Show . . . Trump as himself, made a pass at Giuliani, who was playing a woman. . . . 'You know, you're really beautiful,' Trump told Giuliani's character, who wore a dress and a blonde wig. . . . Trump buried his face in Giuliani's neck and breasts. . . . Asking Trump to 'come on to Rudy' did not seem like a stretch. . . . .'I [Elliot Cuker, the show's director] did not tell him to kiss his breast. He did that himself.' - Michael Kranish and Marc Fisher, *Trump Revealed: An American Journey of Ego, Money, and Power*, New York: Scribner 2016, 265

"Jim, come to dinner tomorrow" said Trump to Comey over the phone.

"Sure. I'll bring my wife."

"I want to be alone with you."

When Comey entered the White House Green Room, two figures were present: Trump and Cupid. Cupid had been assigned to the White House after the Stormy Daniels story broke and Melania had moved out.

Whenever Cupid complained, he was told in no uncertain terms that Trump "had needs," and he was either the god of sex or he was fired. "Frankly," he'd told his mother Venus, the goddess of love, that if she were so interested in Trump's love life, she might "take one for the team so to speak." The result was an 8.1 scale earthquake in Ankara. It is a bad day for humanity when a god is sick. While Trump sat at a small table and leered lasciviously, Cupid flew overhead shooting arrows. A huge flat split screen pictured the Cosby trial and naked images of Melania. Urine droplets collected from Russian prostitutes sprinkled from ceiling fire extinguishers.

"Sit down," said Trump to Comey. "Have I ever told you that you have beautiful eyes?" He reached up a tiny hand and touched Comey's head. "Your hair is great too. But not as great as my hair."

Trump dimmed the lights and lit scented candles. "Do you want to keep your job?" he asked.

"Yes."

"I need loyalty. I expect loyalty," said Trump as he pointed to a loveseat.

"I am the F.B.I. director. Your behavior is improper."

"Not at all. I signed an Executive Order to rename the F.B.I. It is now called Friends Becoming Intimate. We're friends. Right, Jim?"

"Yes. I think we're friends."

"Good. Then you can become director of the new agency I established. It's called the T.B.I., the Trump Bureau of Investigation. The T.B.I. is completely under my control.

The new bureau will not give a shit about Russian ambassador Sergey Kislyak." Trump pursed his small mouth. "For our purposes, 'kiss' is the most important part of 'Kislyak.' Kissing is much more fun than investigating my meetings with Kislyak. If you want to keep your job, kiss me while we sit on the loveseat."

"I will report you to my superior, Attorney General Jefferson Beauregard Sessions III."

"Sessions. That is exactly what I want from you. Let's have a session now."

Comey could take no more. Citing stomach problems, he returned to his office and phoned the attorney general. "I can't be alone with Trump. I need protection. My honor depends on it. What should I do?"

"Back where I come from we have a solution to this here little old lecher problem. Our good southern women sit on verandahs sipping mint juleps while battin' their ever lovin' eyes at potential beaux. While doing so, they're protected by chaperones, their mammies."

"Where can I find a mammy chaperone?"

"Close your eyes. Count to ten. Then open your eyes."

When Comey opened his eyes, he saw a portly woman wearing a long aproned dress and a headscarf. In other words, he was looking dead on at Hattie McDaniel playing Mammy.

"I saw the way Trump treated you and it ain't fittin'. It ain't fittin', I say," said McDaniel before she stopped speaking when she caught sight of herself in Trump's mirror.

She ripped off her scarf and apron. She grabbed scissors from Trump's desk and cut her dress bottom so that it hit her knee. "I will help you as myself, not in my Mammy role. I have played my last maid."

"Trump summoned me back to the White House tonight," said Comey. "Please accompany me."

Comey and McDaniel were alone in the Green Room. To provide further protection from Trump's advances, Comey resorted to a disguise. He pulled down green velvet drapes and wrapped them around himself. The gold curtain rod was perched across his shoulders parallel to the floor. Standing next to McDaniel, Comey tried to be unobtrusive when Trump and his entourage entered the room. His effort failed.

"Seeing you in drag turns me on more," said Trump. "Sure it is impossible for me to grab your nonexistent pussy. No matter. It would have been too high for me to reach anyway."

"The drapes ain't fittin'," shouted McDaniel. "You can't treat this man so badly."

"Nothin' about me is fittin'," snarled Trump. "Now everyone except Comey get the hell outta here."

Trump looked directly into Comey's eyes. "I must have you. You know, you're really beautiful," said Trump as he buried his face in Comey's chest. Comey reached under the drape and took a whistle out of his pocket. He blew the whistle hard to ward off Trump.

In response to the whistle blowing, another *zaftig* woman materialized. She was wearing a large hat.

"My New Yawk mouth is bigger than your New Yawk mouth, Trump. And I mean that figuratively and literally. A woman's place is in the house. That means the White House. Hillary should be in here, not you. And stop comin' on to Comey," shouted Bella Abzug.

"I need loyalty," Trump shouted back.

"I will never be loyal to you," shouted Ethel Merman who had just materialized. Anything you can scream I can belt louder. I can belt anything louder than you. Yes I can."

"I'm with Ethel. Who the hell would want to be loyal to you, you big fat orange outrage lying lout?" said Abzug vociferously. Leave this man alone. Comey, come with me."

Comey exited the White House flanked by Merman and Abzug. He was saved by the Bella. Knowing that the Mammy role was untenable in contemporary America, McDaniel decided to put an updated version of the role to good use. Deciding to serve as a chaperone for a man, she stayed on in the White House to make sure that Trump did not commit sexual assault.

Cupid shot an arrow at Melania. It did not work. Melania loved Trump's money, not Trump. In relation to

Trump, even Cupid has his limitations.

In the age of social media, chaperones have their limitations too: "He's tweeted at me probably fifty times. I've been gone for a year. I'm like the breakup he can't get over. He gets up in the morning. I'm out there living my best life and he gets up in the morning and tweets at me" [James Comey, *The Late Show with Stephen Colbert*, CBS, April 17, 2018].

The Donald and I

or

The Free Hillary Resistance Movement Strikes Back

Professor Sondra Lear was grading papers in her office when the phone rang.

"Professor Lear? This is the Gold House calling."

"The Gold House? Why would the Gold House phone me?"

"The Donald wishes to hire you to tutor the multitudinous young children he fathered during his seven years in office. Will you accept this offer? Your salary will be huge."

"Absolutely not. I am a feminist who recoiled when Trump instituted polygamy in the Gold House because Melania got older. How could I approve of his marriages to twenty-five twenty-five-year old Eastern European beauty queens? He dehumanized these women when he renamed them. The media obsessively focuses on the doings of Aelania, Belania, Celania, Delania, etc. I don't care what color toenail polish Xelania wears. I am a feminist scholar who is an active member of the Free Hillary Resistance Movement. I couldn't believe that the Republicans really did lock Hillary up. I'm hopeful that the F.H.R.M. will eventually break Hillary out of Rikers Island."

"Your decision disappoints me," said the caller. There was a pause, the sound of turning pages, and as if a script was being read, the caller started up again. "Think about the children, Professor Lear. Little Count, Marquis, Chevalier,

Imanka, Ikanka, Harry Winston, Cartier and all their siblings need you. Think about the twins Dauphin and Dauphine. Most of The Donald's offspring are entering pre-school. They will be called upon to continue the Trump dynasty. Smart women still exist; the kids will have to cope with them. What if extraterrestrials from a feminist separatist planet land on the Gold House lawn? You are the perfect tutor to help Trump's children deal with feisty female Earthlings and potential feminist extraterrestrials."

Sondra's revolutionary nature kicked in. She reasoned that she could further F.H.R.M. goals by residing in the Gold House. Trump caused all usual executive branch rules, including presidential succession dictums, to be thrown by the wayside. Presidential protocol becomes irrelevant when the president does not act presidential. Even the very word "president" is obsolete. Russia had the Czar; Germany had the Kiser; Iran had the Shah; America has The Donald. The chief executive is now addressed as "Mr. The Donald." At the State of the Union Address, the Sargent at Arms announces "Mr. Speaker, The Donald of the United States."

"You said the offer was huge," said Sondra. "How huge?" She listened. "Yes," she said. "That's huge." And because Sondra was fed up with Trump, and she liked huge offers, she said yes to the Gold House.

Trump Force One carried Sondra to Washington. Upon arrival, she was whisked into a helicopter. While hovering over the Gold House Rose Garden, she saw the gigantic red, white, and blue blinking neon "TRUMP" sign positioned above the South Portico. The gold painted mansion was too gaudy for Sondra's tastes. But nothing prepared her for the change in the interior.

The Red Room, the Blue Room, and the Vermeil Room (formerly often called the Gold Room), had been transformed into the Gold Rooms. Sondra wondered if James Bond's nemesis Goldfinger had served as the interior decorator. Diamond encrusted doors and marble floors were general all over the Gold House. Cherub-sodden bases supported the gilded furniture. Just as Sondra was reaching for her sunglasses to shield her eyes from the light bouncing off the glitz, Head Wife Melania appeared and extended her hand.

"In accordance with my duties as Head Wife to The Donald, I welcome you to the Gold House," she said. "I and my fellow wives need to expand our horizons. We have agreed to force ourselves to read feminist theory. We appreciate your efforts to teach our children how successfully to closely encounter smart women. The children will certainly need to be prepared for the possibility of feminist extraterrestrials landing on the Gold House lawn. But enough talk about the future. I would like you to meet The Donald's children and some of his other wives."

Two ushers opened the diamond studded golden doors. To the tune of "Hail to the Chief," a single file line of adorable children paraded in front of Sondra, bowed their heads, and walked back while still facing her. One girl broke out of the line, ran forward, and threw her arms around Sondra's knees. "Please, Dr. Sondra. Please be my teacher. I know that women exist who have careers and who don't wear stilettos. You're the first one I've ever met. I want to learn how to be like you. I hate makeup."

Sondra's heart melted. "I will enjoy getting to know you, getting to know all about you," she said to the assembled children.

In short order Sondra's Gold House pedagogy was on the way to becoming effective. Trump's wives were dutifully placing copies of articles written by Hélène Cixous, Donna Haraway, Judith Butler, and Luce Irigary in their designer handbags. True, the wives were not yet reading the articles. Sondra nonetheless viewed feminist theory texts ensconced within Gucci bags as a great leap forward.

As for the children, they enjoyed having fiction written by Joanna Russ, Octavia E. Butler, and Marge Piercy read to them as bedtime stories. The girl who embraced Sondra shared her dream of living on Russ's feminist separatist planet Whileaway. She loved the fact that Whileaway denizens would not be caught dead wearing stilettos. In a defiant act to achieve normalcy, due to Sondra's influence, she demanded to change her name from "Barroness" to "Eleanor."

Sondra was busy teaching Trump's wives and children to the extent that she had yet to meet him. This situation changed when he made an appointment to discuss her progress. She sat next to him on a golden Gold Rooms couch.

"Bloomberg got a third term as mayor. Even if he is richer than me and called me insane, if he can do it, I can do it. I want a third term. But my female voter problem is worse than ever. Women don't like the leader of the free world having a harem. They say that I called Obama a Muslim and now I have a harem. No woman in this country, not one, will vote for me. Not with Hillary locked up and Elizabeth Warren running against me. Pocahontas will not cause Trump's last stand. I love the feminists. I even love the potential feminist extraterrestrials. I need to ingratiate myself to women in general and feminists in particular. Do you have any ideas?" Trump said.

"We can have a party."

"A party?"

"Yes. We should invite feminist theorists to the Gold House to meet your wives."

"I know how to find Eastern European super model wives. But where am I gonna round up American feminists?"

"The Science Fiction Research Association is meeting in Washington next week. I can invite my feminist colleagues as well as scholars from local universities. I will somehow accomplish mission impossible. I will enable feminists to feel comfortable with your wives."

"Feminists mixing with my wives? How can I negotiate an impossible deal like that?"

"Very simple. We need to cater to the feminists."

"You mean feed them Purina Feminist Chow?"

"Offer them a lovely gluten free vegan repast; k.d. lang can provide the music. Your wives need to undergo sartorial metamorphosis." Lelania and Kelania walked in wearing micro miniskirts and gold metallic bras. "They can't dress like this. Lelania and Kelania is not wearing enough clothes.

First rule of hosting a feminist soiree: no visible vaginas. Visible vaginas are a feminist soiree no no. Ditto for grabbing feminist theorists' pussies."

"I see your point. Make a shopping list and give it to the chief butler. What are we going to have for dessert?"

"Pie with ice cream."

"How many scoops will each person get?"

"One."

"I want two scoops."

"Why?"

"Because I'm the president, the most huge and powerful big deal on Earth."

"Okay, you can have two scoops," said Sondra as she gleefully contemplated the president's rising cholesterol levels.

Sondra ordered the most fattening ice cream in the world. We're talking chocolate crunch rocky road cookie dough peanut butter cheese cake Häagen-Dazs topped with bacon sprinkles served in a taco shell bowl. To make sure that the fat content would saturate Trump's arteries, she arranged to give him three scoops. She then stocked up on enough pantsuits, Birkenstocks, and hair scrunchies for the wives. During the party, the wives, dutifully attired in their new clothes, exchanged pleasantries with the assembled feminist theorists. Pelania, who had studied her feminist texts, had a moment of triumph when an assistant professor asked her to name her favorite Cixous article.

"The Laugh of the Medusa," Pelania said emphatically. "I can see the Medusa from my house. From my bathroom to be exact. When my hair gets tangled in the shower, I don't think it's a laughing matter." The assistant professor did not laugh. Pelania wanted to tell Sondra that she knew the correct feminist answer—and to ask for advice.

"Dr. Lear, I got a Cixous question right," said Pelania. "I need to confide in you. I do not love The Donald. I love one of the Secret Service agents. I have been secretly meeting him. This is very dangerous. It is hard to sneak past the head White House eunuchs, Kellyanne Conway and Sarah

Huckabee Sanders. What should I do? I'm already in big trouble because I told my daughter about Mrs. Roosevelt and she decided to change her name to Eleanor."

"I can create a diversion by organizing a Gold House event involving reading my essay on space in *Uncle Tom's Cabin*. You can leave unnoticed when the reading causes everyone to fall asleep. Don't look now but Trump is coming this way." Sondra took the bull by the horns and confronted Trump. "Pelania does not love you," Sondra directly said. "What would you do if you found out that she was having sex with a Secret Service agent?"

"I would have her whipped."

"You're a barbarian."

"I said 'shipped,' not 'whipped.' I will send Pelania on a nice cruise. These concubines. They wear me out. I can use a break. But let's talk about this 'bigly' party. You did an amazing job. Great ice cream. I had four scoops. Too bad if everyone else had only one. My wives are still hot in Birkenstocks," Trump said. In a manner as abrupt as his manic conversation shifts, he held out his arms. "Shall we dance?"

There was a limit to how far Sondra could go—even to benefit the F.H.R.M. Relying on her inner Scheherazade, she tried to talk to gain time.

"We share so many things in common. I'm from Queens too. I grew up in Forest Hills, straight down Queens Boulevard from your childhood home in Jamaica Estates. I used to see your father's 'Trump Pavilion' sign located next to the Van Wyck Expressway."

Trump ignored what Sondra said and stepped in. He placed his arm around her waist. Since she did not want to insult him and ruin all of her efforts on behalf of the F.H.R.M., she had to dance with him.

"Sondra, let's make a deal. Marry me. Become my twenty-seventh wife. Marrying a feminist professor would be huge for my re-election success. You can have Pelania's room. Whadaya say?"

"I say 'never.' You know very well that Jewish women from Forest Hills do not become the twenty-seventh wife of anyone. Furthermore, fat orange haired men in their late seventies are not my type."

Eleanor ran into the room. "Dr. Sondra, come quick. A flying saucer has landed on the Gold House lawn," she screamed.

"Not to worry, Eleanor. This is a job for a super science fiction scholar."

Sondra made her way to the Gold House lawn where she closely encountered little green women walking down a flying saucer's gangplank. They wore silver pantsuits, Birkenstocks, and scrunchies. "Take us to your leader," they said in unison. "We want to meet her."

"I have no doubt that you're feminist extraterrestrials," Sondra confidently stated. "Let me calmly cut to the chase. Americans are in deep trouble. Our leader is a bombastic male chauvinist pig carnival barker con man whose ego is larger than the entire universe. Believe me. You do not want to be taken to him. Will you help Americans?"

"Yes," the feminist extraterrestrials said in unison.

"Terrific. And not a moment too soon. Hillary, America's rightful female leader, has been locked up. Trump, that's the name of our male leader, is on the cusp of winning a third term. By the way, I'm Professor Sondra Lear."

One of the little green women extended her tentacle toward Sondra. "Nice to meet you. I'm Captain Xyra. Here we come to save the day. That means that mighty feminist extraterrestrials are on the way. Exactly what can we do for you? We have extraordinary reality altering powers."

"First thing is to break Hillary out of Rikers."

"Done," Captain Xyra said as Hillary materialized on the White House lawn wearing an orange prison jumpsuit.

Sondra saw Hillary and became unnerved. "No. This is not right," she said to Xyra. "Hillary wears designer pantsuits, not prison jumpsuits. Turn her jumpsuit into a pantsuit. Make it black. Black needs to be the new orange for Hillary. Oh and she needs sunglasses"

"Done."

"Perfect. Now Hillary can join the party and blend in with the other feminist attendees." Sondra turned toward Hillary. "I'm an active F.H.R.M. member who could not be happier to meet you. Join the Gold House party for feminist scholars and Trump's wives. The sunglasses will allow you to be incognito. Have a drink. Enjoy yourself while the feminist extraterrestrials and I figure out how to ensconce you in your rightful place as president of the United States."

"I will accept your advice," said Hillary. "Despite my wonkiness, feminist extraterrestrials are beyond my purview." Hillary walked into the Gold House hoping that she could transform it back into the White House of yore. Sondra turned toward Xyra.

"I know exactly what to do," Sondra said. "I can accomplish my objective without any extraterrestrial intervention. I will simply use your presence to my advantage. I need you to do one more thing. Please make everyone on Earth—with the exception of me and Trump - forget that the little green women landing on the Gold House lawn thing ever happened.

"Done," said Xyra. "We will be flying off now. Great to meet you, Sondra."

Sondra's plan involved allowing Trump to be Trump. She walked into the party and approached Hillary.

"Hillary, please remove your sunglasses. Tell Trump that you are here and call the police."

Police entered the Gold Room. "Lock her up," screamed Trump. "Lock crooked Hillary back up. Do ya know how she got out? I'll tell ya how she got out. Feminist extraterrestrials got her out. That's how. Feminist extraterrestrials landed on the Gold House lawn a few minutes ago. There were all these huge little green women. Little green women are ugly. I will build a wall around the Gold House to keep out the ugly huge little green women. I had enough trouble with the Mexicans and the Muslims. Now I gotta contend with the little green women. Maybe gun owners could do something about the little green women - and Hillary too."

Men in white coats arrived in what immediately again would be called the White House. They placed Trump in a straitjacket. He ended up back in New York, in Bellevue Hospital. Sondra enjoyed hearing k.d. lang do a rendition of "Hail to the Chief" as Hillary was sworn in as president of the United States. The long national Trump nightmare was over

Hillary was the first of many female presidents. Elizabeth Warren succeeded her. Amy Schumer, following in her relative Senator Chuck Schumer's political footsteps, went, in the manner of Reagan, from show business to the White House.

Due to Sondra's influence, Eleanor Trump was by far the most effective woman president. Eleanor (called E.T.) was the first American president to visit a feminist planet. E.T. and Xyra got along famously. Eleanor gave a party for Xyra in the White House. Both women wore white pantsuits, Birkenstocks—and scrunchies. They each enjoyed two scoops of fat free vanilla ice cream.

I Am Trump the Great and Powerful

Professor Sondra Lear was coping with denial regarding the catastrophe, incompetence, and idiocy characterizing Trump's administration. Helpless in the face of this new reality, she knew that she had to turn to alternative fantasy story facts. Her scholarly expertise provided the only solution to the advent of the Trump presidency.

Sondra defined Trump as a tower-dwelling con artist wizard who fits the stock fantasy story villainous protagonist bill. According to fantasy's garden-variety structuralist poetics, in order to quash Trump, Sondra had to access his tower. She abruptly turned back to reality to accomplish her objective.

Trump had instituted a new government agency: the Department of Misogyny. Since Sondra had spent her academic career being a feminist theorist, it was obvious that, according to Trump regime logic, she was the perfect person to head this department. After all, Trump had appointed a racist to be attorney general, a public education opponent to serve as secretary of education, and a pollution lover to run the Environmental Protection Agency. It made perfect sense for him to tap a feminist to lead the Department of Misogyny. After Sondra sent Trump her lengthy vita which listed her myriad feminist publications, she was immediately granted an interview.

Sondra, who was attractive enough to meet Trump's appearance qualifications for female employees, prepared for the interview by disguising herself as a Republican woman. She put on a long straight haired blonde wig, a too tight suit, spike heels, and too much makeup. Taking her little dachshund Lassie in hand, Sondra prepared to leave her Manhattan apartment to follow Fifth Avenue's grey concrete sidewalk to the deplorable wizard of ours' tower.

Sondra and Lassie went down to her building's lobby and greeted the doorman, a man named Moe who was both a Muslim and an immigrant. When Sondra told Moe that she and Lassie were off to see the wizard in order to use her feminist credentials to head the Department of Misogyny, he said that her idea was brilliant. He was disappointed that, because he had to flee his country and interrupt his education, he was not smart enough to help her with her plan. Sondra, surmising that Trump should have the opportunity finally to meet a working class Muslim, invited Moe to join her. Sondra, Moe, and Lassie set off down the grey concrete sidewalk to see the con artist wizard.

They did not have a long way to go to reach Trump Tower. While standing in front of Bergdorf Goodman, they looked in the store's front window and saw a female mannequin waving at them. Leaving Lassie in Moe's care, Sondra entered the store and approached the mannequin. "Why are you waving at me?" she asked.

"I am an advanced form of artificial intelligence endowed with super intuitive powers. More simply stated, I am an android from the future who recognizes that you are a liberal feminist dressed in Republican clothing."

Despite her clearly brilliant observation, the mannequin seemed to be lacking something.

"Are you a liberal feminist too?" Sondra asked. As an expert in science fiction, Sondra treated every encounter with time travelers as an opportunity to learn.

"I am not sure," said the android. "I don't have a heart so I don't know how I feel."

"You should come with me to see the con artist wizard. He might get you a better job. A lot of people he hires don't have hearts."

"Can your feminist science fiction expertise be used to help me to attain a heart?" asked the android. "I do not want a job. As a time travelling android, I know the impending horror Trump will unleash. It's not a pretty picture."

"You are welcome to join me, Moe, and Lassie. Maybe becoming a member of our group will somehow enable you to acquire a heart."

Sondra and her companions soon came face to face with a carriage horse. "Can a talking horse come along with you too?" asked the horse. "I lack the courage to speak up for myself and say that it is cruel to force horses to pull carriages. And, oh, my name is Ms. Ed."

Lassie, seeing that a fellow animal was in distress, responded with a welcoming woof. With the permission of the carriage driver who was surprised to learn that his horse could talk, Sondra removed Ms. Ed's harness. She promised to help the horse find the courage to speak. The driver, who now considered a feminist talking horse to be a professional liability, was glad to get rid of Ms. Ed by giving her to Sondra.

Soon everyone was standing right smack in front of Trump Tower. They saw a woman who looked like a mirror image of Sondra attired in a Republican woman costume flying overhead on a broom. "It's Kellyanne Conway. She was born in New Jersey. In geographical relation to New York City, she's the Wicked Witch of the West" said Sondra to her companions.

Kellyanne circled above the group as, using her broom's exhaust pipe emissions, she wrote "Surrender Sondra" above Trump Tower. "I'll get you, Sondra. I'll get you and your little dog too. Ditto for your doorman, android, and talking horse," the wicked witch screamed.

"And exactly how are you going to accomplish that?" responded Sondra. "I am a science fiction scholar. Whatever evil witchcraft you can unleash, I can wield the literary tropes needed to nullify it."

"Deal with my army of flying rats," screamed Kellyanne. Myriad uniformed rats suddenly appeared in the broom's wake.

Sondra turned to the android who just happened to be equipped with heat vision. As red hot beams emanated from her eyes, multitudinous flying rat corpses were soon strewn over the grey concrete sidewalk. They were rapidly removed by their less glamorous cousins, sewer rats.

"Very impressive," shrieked Kellyanne. "But before you enter Trump Tower, you must fulfill one requirement."

"Which is?" Sondra inquired.

"Bring me one of Hillary's pantsuits."

Sondra texted the Democratic National Committee. A FedEx truck soon delivered the required garment. Sondra unwrapped the box, threw the white Ralph Lauren designed pantsuit at Kellyanne, and entered the Trump Tower elevator with her companions in tow. When the doors swooshed open in a manner Sondra, as a science fiction expert, could appreciate, she and her group exited and were met by a big giant weirdly coiffed orange head hologram. "I am Trump, the great and powerful. Who are you?" thundered the head.

"I am Professor Sondra Lear, the eminent feminist science fiction theorist. Big giant outrageous orange head, know that I am here to interview for the Department of Misogyny headship."

"I don't know from what 'misogyny' means. Nor have I ever met a feminist scholar. But you're good looking enough, Sondra. I would rate you eight point five. Wonderful straight blonde hair, tight suit, heels, and make-up. You're hired," thundered the orange head.

Lassie, fascinated by a shimmering gold curtain, took an edge in her mouth and pulled it aside. The group saw what was behind the curtain: a tall fat man wearing a baggy suit who was frantically pulling levers on a hologram projection machine.

"Consider yourself demystified—even though you don't know what the word means," said Sondra. "Trump, you are not great. You are powerful only because you adroitly manipulate a propaganda machine by lying and making false promises. What is both great and powerful is the impact of story—and I am in charge of this one. You made up alternative facts. Well, now you have to deal with alternative fantasy story facts. The great and powerful impact of story will give you a lesson about how truly to improve lives."

Sondra turned to Ms. Ed. "You are no ordinary horse. You can phone Mayor de Blasio and tell him that carriage horses should not be abused. True, cellphones are not made for horses. But I can punch in the appropriate New York City government phone number for you," said Sondra. Ms. Ed found the courage to tell the mayor exactly how she felt. De Blasio, impressed by the opportunity to converse with a talking horse, declared that it was illegal to use carriage horses. All the horses were set free to frolic in Central Park's Sheep Meadow where they spent their days producing fertilizer to be used in urban rooftop farming initiatives. Carriage drivers were given wheelbarrows and shovels and the opportunity to ensure that the farms were well supplied. "The android is much more powerful than you, Trump," Sondra continued. "Although, unlike you, she lacks a flesh and blood heart, you are the one who is truly heartless. The android will use her superior future-based technological prowess to automate all the city's lobbies in order to make doormen unnecessary. She will accomplish this innovation free of charge. The mayor will mandate that doormen will still receive their salaries to enable them to attend the City University of New York. My doorman has already enrolled in Baruch College's M.B.A. program." Sondra looked at Moe. "You have always been smart," she said.

"I have to interrupt," said the android. "I will violate the Prime Directive and tell you one thing that will ensue in the future. Moe became disenchanted with business and switched to science. He discovered a cure for cancer. In the face of this real future fact, Trump I dare you to continue your diatribes and bans against Muslims."

"What is going to happen to Trump?" asked the now courageous Ms. Ed. As soon as she finished her sentence, a huge hot air balloon appeared floating above Trump Tower.

"Ms. Ed., Trump will go somewhere over the rainbow far away in this beautiful balloon," declared Sondra. "Trump, you will spend eternity grabbing wicked witches' pussies. And, although you will fail to catch the reference, no comparison with T. S. Eliot's *Old Possum's Book of Practical Cats* is intended."

Trump found himself crouching in the ascending balloon's basket. A huge rainbow appeared over Trump Tower. Trump floated somewhere over the rainbow.

Hillary suddenly appeared wearing the pantsuit FedEx had delivered to Kellyanne. Afraid to confront the alternative fantasy story facts which caused Trump to float away, Congress and the Supreme Court admitted that the election had been a huge mistake after all. They proclaimed that the popular vote winning Hillary was the rightful president of the United States.

Sondra congratulated President Clinton. She picked up Lassie and walked along the grey concrete sidewalk back to her apartment. "The alternative fantasy story fact is that there's no place like home in my real Trumpless country," she said to herself as she put her key in the door.

Wombville

or

Feminist Extraterrestrials Build A Worldwide Subway Web

There are no glimmers of possible federal aid for the city's [New York] troubled mass transit system, far and away the largest in the country and, as such, important for the national economy. Nothing has been offered [by the Trump administration] to build a sorely needed rail tunnel under the Hudson River connecting New Jersey and Manhattan. - Editorial Board, "Hometown Boy Doesn't Make Good," *New York Times,* August 5, 2017, A18

Professor Sondra Lear could not stand Trump for another minute. Positioning satire as her most effective resistance tactic, she deviated from writing scholarly articles to becoming a Trump story creating woman warrior. She had just finished a takedown of newly minted White House communications director Anthony Scaramucci. As a native New Yorker, she had nailed his Long Island vernacular and hyper masculine New York douche bag demeanor. And, lo, eleven days into his White House gig, Scaramucci was fired. Sondra's fiction could not keep pace with Trump regime reality. Despite spending her professional life contemplating feminist separatist planets, her imagination failed in the face of Trump world absurdity.

Sondra ripped up the suddenly dated story and

opened her refrigerator intending to drown out her sorrows by ingesting an entire Häagen-Dazs chocolate ice cream pint as quickly as Trump fired White House staff members. She saw a note attached to the pint. "Dear Sondra," it read. "I am contacting you because you are a feminist alien expert. The big giant maternal head who governs my home world, the feminist separatist planet Friedania, is concerned about Earth. She had a hissy fit because a bombastic orange outrage defeated brilliant Hillary Clinton. The Head sent me to Earth as her emissary to help women unite and quash patriarchy. Friedanians have powers and abilities far beyond the reach of Earthlings—even your entire military industrial complex. Please meet me on the Empire State Building's Observation Deck. I want to tell you about the big giant maternal head's plan to change Earth into a unified feminist utopia. Hope to see you soon. Yours sincerely, Shyra, Friedanian Emissary Assigned to Earth."

Sondra could not refuse Shyra's offer. Fraternizing with a feminist extraterrestrial would cause Sondra to become the envy of the entire Science Fiction Research Association. Ignoring the fact that this experience would put Sondra out of business because feminist extraterrestrials would no longer be science fictional, she threw professional caution to the wind and made her way to the Empire State Building.

Upon arrival on the Observation Deck, she saw a tall rainbow skinned woman wearing a gold jumpsuit and thigh high gold boots.

"Pleased to meet you," said the feminist alien. "I'm Shyra."

"Your red, orange, yellow, green, blue, indigo, and violet skin is certainly eye catching," Sondra replied.

"Friedanians resemble giant roaches. I have assumed this guise to make you comfortable. Since you are a New Yorker and as such you are used to battling roaches, I did not want you to come after me with a Raid can in hand. My skin color symbolizes South Africa, the Rainbow Nation. The big giant maternal head is very impressed with that country's nonviolent revolution. She applauds the various black and white tribes who are overcoming their cultural differences and trying to unify. The same is true of the French and English Canadians. But South Africa is more exciting than Canada, even from an extraterrestrial standpoint. Will you accompany me to South Africa, my chosen base of operations for establishing a feminist borderless governmental system on Earth?"

"Certainly. But how long will I be away? I have to cancel my subscription to the *New York Times* and arrange for someone to cover my feminist science fiction class."

"Not to worry. I will alter the space time continuum so that no one will notice your absence."

"Can we go to South Africa in your spaceship? After reading about so many spaceships, it would be great to fly in one."

"Sure. My spaceship is parked in Antarctica. The ship was dented when an ice shelf chunk broke off. Spaceship parking is hard to come by."

"As a Manhattan resident, I can relate to parking problems. How will we get to Antarctica?"

"We can take the subway."

"The 6 train is located near my apartment. But it only goes as far south as lower Manhattan."

"Friedanians have just completed a huge infrastructure project, a subway which unites every location on Earth. We initiated this transportation improvement because the New York subway is a model for social, cultural, and national boundary unity. People from all over your world peacefully coexist in the subway. In order to travel from point A to point B in New York, everyone crams in and braves odors, rats, potential breakdown and god—that's an Earth god, Friedanians are atheists—knows what. Our technology makes it possible for everyone on Earth to avail themselves of an inclusive global subway network. Here are a parka and boots. We can access the Friedanian subway at the mundane 34th Street station."

New Yorkers, who are used to seeing everything, were

unfazed when their rush hour commute included closely encountering a rainbow skinned alien dressed in gold accompanied by someone carrying a down jacket and snow boots in July. Shyra and Sondra walked down the ramp leading to the B, D, and F trains as Sondra tried to ignore the giant rat chomping on a pizza slice. When Shyra touched the station's southern back wall, a golden door appeared. The "women" passed through the door and entered a pristine subway station whose ceiling was encrusted with diamonds. As Sondra stepped within a platinum subway train which arrived on silver tracks, she said "I don't think that I am in New York anymore." Faster than a New York minute, Sondra looked out of the subway car's window and read the station sign which said "Antarctica."

"We're here," announced Shyra. The "women" detrained, rode an escalator, and walked out of the Antarctica station on to packed ice. Sondra noticed a spaceship which was a dead ringer for the Klingon Bird-of-Prey used on *Star Trek*. "We could have taken the subway all the way to South Africa. But arriving in a spaceship is much more impressive," said Shyra as she sat in the captain's chair. "The ship is set on automatic pilot to land in Cape Town on Table Mountain whose flat top makes a perfect spaceship landing pad."

A crowd gathered as Shyra and Sondra emerged from the ship. International media soon arrived. Trump tweeted that his Inauguration Day crowd was bigger than the Cape Town crowd.

"I come in peace accompanied by an Earth woman," stated Shyra. "She is a New Yorker—and a feminist science fiction scholar—so she can deal with this situation. I will try to talk as fast as she does to explain why I am here. I am an emissary sent by the big giant maternal head of the feminist separatist planet Friedania. Your patriarchal governmental system replete with artificial national boundaries is no longer sustainable. In light of having first contact with an extraterrestrial, your geographical designations—such as North Korea and South Korea, mainland China and Taiwan, and even Soho and Noho in Manhattan—make no sense. All humans need to join together and form a unified political entity. Using Friedania as a model, women should be in charge of Earth. Professor Lear, please explain how best to accomplish this objective."

"As an English professor, I can provide the perfect answer," stated Sondra. "Marshall McLuhan said that we live in a 'global village.' Communications technology keeps making the village smaller. It is time to get rid of national designations and use one global village appellation to rename Earth. I suggest 'Wombville.' Every human emanates from a womb. 'Wombville' imbues people with commonality and celebrates women's generative power. Women will of course run the singular global Wombville government."

"Great ideas," said Shyra. "But how are you going to accomplish female rule? Surely you don't expect men to cooperate. I can't imagine, say, your Trump and Putin happily resigning."

"Appealing to logic is the way to begin. We can point to what United States Senators Susan Collins and Lisa Murkowski accomplished in regard to saving millions of Americans from having their health insurance rescinded. In my opinion, every sane person on Earth recognizes that the world would now be a much better place if Hillary had been elected president of the United States. Thoughtful women are crucial to human success. Who, for example, can fault Queen Elizabeth's unifying capabilities? Golda Meir was not chopped liver. If logic fails, I can again put on my English professor hat—no Trump supporter red cap which says 'Make America Great Again'—and arrive at a text-based solution. What I have in mind is both textual and sexual. In the manner of 'Lysistrata' protagonists, women can band together and refuse to have sex with men."

Logic failed.

Shyra made it possible for every woman on Earth voluntarily to wear a chastity belt. Since men capitulated in twenty-four hours, this peaceful revolution rivaled the South African one. Earth's big giant maternal head came to power immediately.

The head, which was attached to a white pantsuit wearing body, had a short blonde coif. Hillary had taken the subway from New York to Cape Town. She was impressed by being able to arrive in South Africa in a New York minute. After taking the big giant maternal head oath of office, Hillary announced that she wanted to share her global leadership position with diverse women. She explained that several heads are better than one and invited Angela Merkel and the reincarnated Winnie Madikizela-Mandela to become co-heads. Hillary established a head advisory council which consisted of former male leaders' wives—with the exception of Melania Trump. Melania, who could only offer posing nude as her most important work experience, was not qualified to be a council member. After Hillary put her staff in place, she asked Shyra to provide enough blue baseball caps emblazoned with a "W" for everyone on Earth. The "W" stood for Wombville in particular and women in general.

Shyra told Hillary how to access the worldwide subway web: "Touch any wall while thinking lovely global community thoughts. A door which leads to a subway station will appear in the wall. When you board a train, think about your destination and the humanity you share with the people who live there."

The dispersing Table Mountain crowd welcomed the opportunity to exchange their national designations for global citizenship. Even though the desire to take the subway to anywhere knew no bounds, the system remained uncrowded.

Sondra began to bid Shyra adieu. "May I travel back to New York with you in your spaceship?"

"I view spaceships in the manner of your attitude toward horse drawn carriages. They are antiquated. I took a spaceship out of the Friedanian Transportation Museum because, well, Earthlings expect aliens to land in one. First contact is important and I didn't want to disappoint anyone. Friedanians routinely avail themselves of the intergalactic subway. I can instantaneously travel to planets as diverse as de Beauvoir, Cixous, Wollstonecraft, and Greer. But Earthlings are not yet ready to avail themselves of this uber advanced subway technology."

"I understand. I will be glad to take the more basic worldwide subway web home. But first I would like to do some shopping and sightseeing in Cape Town."

After visiting Boulders Beach, which housed nesting penguins, and stocking up on squid sold by street vendors, Sondra made her way to the University of Cape Town's English department office. She walked up Table Mountain which housed grazing wildebeest as well as the campus and entered the department's copy machine room. After paying homage to André Brink and J.M. Coetzee, who had certainly used the copy machine located in that room, she placed her hand on the wall and began to sing. "Getting to know you. Getting to know all about you. Getting to like you. Getting to hope you like me. . . . Because of all the beautiful and new things I'm learning about you day by day." She accessed the subway station, boarded a train, and arrived in New York.

Enlivened by all the beautiful and new things she had learned as a feminist science fiction scholar, Sondra entered her apartment building, picked up the *New York Times* waiting outside her door, and began to prepare her next class. She looked forward to taking the subway to Rome for Italian food and hopping over to Beijing to sample authentic Chinese cuisine. There was no need for her to go to Japan; sushi is basically the same regardless of where you eat it.

Clinton, Madikizela-Mandela, and Merkel were busy running the world. In order to bring the British Commonwealth countries into the Wombville fold, Queen Elizabeth agreed to serve as an honorary council member. In the event of a crisis, the Friedanians made it possible for the council to channel Eleanor Roosevelt and Indira Gandhi. Although the aliens meant well, when they tried to include Cleopatra, confusion resulted. Because Friedanian knowledge of Earth culture was not perfect, they produced Elizabeth Taylor playing Cleopatra rather than Cleopatra herself. This mistake was easily rectified.

The council governed Earth in an organized fashion by designating a specific week to accomplish a specific task at hand. The first such initiative, called Education Week, included the proviso that all universities, a mere subway ride away, would be made be available to all students regardless of where they resided. Conservation Week solved the global warming problem by banning all now obsolete cars, trucks, planes, and mundane trains. Due to the ban, no person would ever again die in a vehicular accent. In terms of further improvement, food, which now could be shipped instantaneously, became more nutritious. The ease of delivering all goods and services raised the world's gross national product.

Because everyone had equal access to the forever replenishing diamond subway station ceiling decorations, poverty was eradicated. Ditto for taxes. Easy global social intercourse eventually resulted in the end of language barriers. Everyone began to speak fluent Womb, whose syntax did not include feminine and masculine forms. The council mandated that violence against women would be punishable by imprisonment in an intergalactic penitentiary. Realizing that Woman and nature were interconnected, council members protected animals by banning factory farms and hunting. Women who hurt women's interests— Kellyanne Conway and Sarah Huckabee Sanders, for example—were banished to the Phantom Zone.

All was going along swimmingly—until war broke out. Trump and Putin, who could not abide the loss of their power, decided to band together. Trump began his onslaught by insisting that Hillary could not be the big giant maternal head because she had used a private email server. He dealt with Merkel and Madikizela-Mandela by proposing to build a wall to corral them within the now no longer extant countries they had come from. He even went so far as to brag that he could grab their pussies. As a last resort, he criticized their appearances by declaring that they were over thirty-five and, hence, worthless because they did not come close to being rated a ten.

Putin hacked into the council's computers and generated fake news about council members. When all else failed, the two deposed leaders launched nuclear weapons. Since this was a crisis beyond the ability of even emergency council members Roosevelt, Gandhi, and Cleopatra to solve, it was necessary to call in the Friedanians; they zapped the missiles out of the sky. Trump and Putin's attempted coup d'état failed. Earth was united by the observation that Wombville solidarity was superior to the patriarchal division Trump and Putin represented. The council used the subway to ship these guys to Siberia. They were sentenced to spending the rest of their lives sitting in an igloo while being forced to watch an endless tape of feminist theory lectures. Trump named his enclosure "Trump Igloo." Melania asked to live in her own private igloo. Putin took to the Siberian tundra on his horse. Since he wouldn't wear a shirt while riding a horse, he was soon found frozen to death, slightly chewed on by badgers.

With the last vestige of patriarchy contained, things were going well in Wombville—until an aspect of human nature which Shyra did not anticipate kicked in. People were taking the subway to the extent that a planet wide obesity problem emerged. The worldwide subway web, in other words, was too efficient. Shyra tweaked the system by mandating that all subway riders had to adhere to eating right and exercising. Failure to do so would result in Global Metro Card surrender until the offender adopted a healthful lifestyle. Weight Watchers membership skyrocketed.

After getting the crisis under control, the council went about its business. Cleopatra proposed that pyramid-shaped computer screens should be used to indicate subway arrival times. Roosevelt, drawing upon her experience establishing the United Nations, was working to get Earthlings up to par for intergalactic subway access. Queen Elizabeth suggested that council members wear tiaras at official functions.

Hillary appointed Sondra to serve as emissary to Friedania. Since Roosevelt had much more to accomplish before Earthlings had the ability to ride the intergalactic subway, Sondra traveled to Friedania via spaceship. She was thrilled to have the opportunity to sit in the captain's chair and beam stuff up. Upon arrival, she was given special sunglasses to prevent Friedanians from looking like roaches.

Emissary Lear was introduced to the Friedanian big giant maternal head—who highly resembled a female Wizard of Oz projection—with great pomp and circumstance. On behalf of all humans, Sondra profusely thanked her for uniting Earth. Sondra's perspective was of course forever changed. For example, even though she was a New Yorker, she could never again stomp on a roach. She imagined that she might be exterminating what she thought a baby Friedanian might look like.

Sondra, however, could carry unity only so far. Like *Fiddler On The Roof* protagonist Tevye the Dairyman—perhaps one of the "local milk people" Trump famously referred to when talking with Australian Prime Minister Malcolm Turnbull—refusing to speak to his third daughter, she had her limits. Sondra could never find commonality with Trump and his supporters. She asked Shyra to close the Siberian subway station. No loss. No one wanted to go there anyway. Trump spent his final days proclaiming that he would make Siberia great again.

No one listened.

Zsa Zsa Trump Makes America Great Again

Professor Sondra Lear initially thought that there was nothing she could do to alter the fact that Trump was president. Her attitude was short lived, though. Sondra, resolving to put her science fiction expertise to good use, wondered if feminist extraterrestrials could rescue liberal American Earthlings from the Orange Outrage. She felt that she should try to contact them.

Sondra made her way to the Empire State Building Observation Deck at twilight and pointed a flashlight toward the sky. "You hoo," shouted Sondra hopefully. "It's me. I have devoted my professional life to studying feminist extraterrestrials. Are you up there? If so, please report to this observation deck immediately if not sooner. Help."

Sondra stopped waving the flashlight, breathed deeply, and gazed at the sky. Nothing happened. She hung her head and walked back to her apartment.

When she opened her refrigerator and reached for the chocolate Häagen-Dazs, she saw the following note pasted to the container: "Dear Professor Lear, Please come to the Feminist Press Office at the City University of New York Graduate Center at four PM tomorrow."

Sondra entered the office and closely encountered a nondescript middle-aged black woman seated at the front desk. She noticed that the woman's hands each contained six fingers.

Are you a feminist extraterrestrial?" Sondra calmly inquired.

"You bet. How did you know? I come from the planet Ovum."

"You have too many fingers."

"Oops. I don't have this human body transformation thing down pat yet. Ovumians, who resemble giant roaches, have to make enormous physical changes at the last minute when they come to New York. Pleased to meet you, Sondra. I'm Zsa Trump."

"What? Zsa Zsa Trump? How can a feminist extraterrestrial be named Zsa Zsa Trump?"

"Very simple. I married Donald Trump."

"No way."

"The marriage occurred in the near future. I traveled back in time to answer your call for help. Melania reached her limit when Trump took Stormy Daniels with him to Moscow. National Public Radio hacked the Russian camera feed. They just used the audio, but she moved out and divorced him. Since it wouldn't have looked right for a man in his mid-seventies to acquire a replacement twenty-something fashion model wife, Trump improved his race relations image by marrying a no longer young black woman. In addition, because Obama had a black wife, Trump wanted one too. He desired to make Obama appear to be less unique. When I materialized in the White House Gold Room, Trump discerned that I fit his new wife bill. He immediately called a clergy person and married me. And, lo and behold, I became Zsa Zsa Trump."

"Why 'Zsa Zsa'? That name is associated with a deceased Hungarian."

"Zsa Zsa Gabor was married to Conrad Hilton. Hilton named one of his sons Barron. So of course did Trump—who used the name 'John Barron' when he promoted himself by assuming the guise of a phony publicist. Trump obviously emulates Hilton. Not to be outdone, the president now also has a son named Barron and a wife named Zsa Zsa."

"That's nice. But how are you benefitting American feminists who are mad as hell and can't take Trump anymore?"

"Easy. Ovumians have taken what you Earthlings call voodoo and imbued it with our extraterrestrial powers and abilities. I am supposedly from Cape Town. People attributed the vast changes they saw in Trump to my claim to be a voodoo priestess."

"How did you successfully change Trump? Even White House chief of staff John F. Kelly, a retired United States Marine Corps general, failed."

"Ovumians can do brain revisions. With a snap of two of my twelve fingers, I altered Trump's brain. I turned him into a sophisticated, measured, reasonable, competent, and articulate intellectual who advocates universal health care."

"You turned Trump into Obama."

"Right."

"As soon as I activated his brain revision, Trump donned a new baseball cap which said 'Make America Green Again.' He fired his unqualified cabinet members and replaced them with experts, mostly women. Turning America into a sanctuary for immigrants and refugees was his greatest humanitarian achievement. He also de-friended Putin on Facebook."

Sondra, satisfied with the changes Zsa Zsa instituted, had one more question for her new extraterrestrial acquaintance.

"Can you give Trump normal hair and make him as svelte as Obama?"

"Sorry. No. Your request exceeds the limits of even Ovumian power."

When Sondra returned home, she carefully put her flashlight in an accessible place. The new Obama-esque Trump was not immortal—especially since he was still fat. Sondra knew that she had to be prepared to take action if Pence became president. She contemplated asking an Ovumian to change Pence into Bill Clinton. Pence would not go to a restaurant with any woman who was not his wife. The potential brain-revised Pence would make exceptions for female White House interns.

Perhaps President Pence would even go one better than Clinton. Sondra imagined that soon after Pence embraced bigamy, an Ovumian named Marilyn Monroe-Pence would become Karen Pence's sister-wife.

Trump Meets Pussy Galore and Is Fit to Be Tied

"The Women's March had a poor showing. Very poor," said Trump. "Only four and a half women showed up in Washington. Six and four eighths women marched in New York. I include the fractions because ugly women—any broad who's less than a ten—don't count. Except when we're talkin' my inauguration where billions of people were packed in like sardines as far as the eye could see. "

"I attended the Women's March and I saw thousands of people. Thousands are definitely more than four and a half," Anderson Cooper said to Kellyanne Conway.

"We're dealing with alternative facts," she calmly answered. "You should know that by now, working for a fake news station and all."

Trump's falsification penchant was initially right on target vis-à-vis what at first resembled an alternative fact in relation to everything humanity had hitherto defined as factual. It wasn't even considered odd when a spaceship landed on the White House lawn. As the hatch opened, an elongated alien emerged. It had a pink furry body accented by a white chest patch, a long tail, and a feminine feline face.

"Take me to your leader," said the alien to a Secret Service agent.

The agent walked into the White House and approached Trump. "Sir, there's an extraterrestrial Pink Panther outside who says that she wants to meet you."

"'She?' Is she hot?" asked Trump. He knew his orange hair went well with the alien's pink fur. "I am meeting a female extraterrestrial. I can't make this up. What should I do?" Trump asked the agent.

"Call a female extraterrestrial expert."

"An expert? I hate experts. My secretary of education never set foot in a public school. My Environmental Protection Agency head hates nature. And I know shit about being the president. Where the hell am I gonna find an extraterrestrial expert?"

"I'll have an intern research the subject."

"Make sure that the intern is hot."

It only took minutes for an intern to arrive and supply the requested information. Trump was disappointed that she wasn't nearly as hot as Ivanka.

"I've located a feminist science fiction scholar named Sondra Lear who teaches at the Metropolitan University of New York. I suggest you contact her," said the intern who handed Trump a phone.

"Professor Lear, this is President Trump," stated the president. "I guess there's no such thing as a hot scholar. In any event, I won the election with a huge landslide. I won by the biggest margin in history. Only two and three quarter women participated in the Women's March."

"Why did you phone and ply me with alternative truths?" asked Sondra.

"I'm stuck here with a ten foot tall pink and white furry huge female extraterrestrial. You're an expert on female extraterrestrials. Who the hell else do ya expect me to call?"

"I see. Is the alien's height measurement a real fact or an alternative fact?"

"It's real. I need your help."

"I have no desire to help you."

"Why not? I'm desperate."

"We're both from Queens. I grew up in Forest Hills which, as you know, is near your childhood home in Jamaica Estates. My older sister Alondra went to the Kew-Forest School with you. You grabbed her pussy in the school cafeteria."

"Oh yeah, I remember Alondra. She was just a seven. I don't grab sevens' pussies. Alondra's lying. I'm dealing with a huge national emergency. Put the fake news pussy grabbing story behind you and get your ass to the White House immediately."

A few hours later, Sondra landed on the White House lawn in a helicopter. She disembarked and extended her hand toward the alien's pink paw.

"My name is Pussy Galore," said the alien.

"Call me Lear, Sondra Lear. On second thought, 'Sondra' will be fine."

"I've been monitoring America and I'm well aware of your president's pussy grabbing penchant," said the alien. "He can't grab my pussy because I don't have one. The denizens of my home planet do not use genitals to reproduce. As for what we do use, well don't ask. You don't want to know. I need to explain another biological difference. I am less warm blooded than humanoids. The bottom line is that I am standing out here freezing. My fur is not keeping me warm."

Sondra handed Pussy Galore a Women's March pussy hat. Pussy Galore put on the pussy hat and smiled. The pink hat exactly matched her pink fur.

"The hat's weird points at the top look like horns," said Trump. "I love the Jews."

"I want to foster female solidarity, Sondra," said Pussy Galore. I can use my reproductive method immediately to generate many more of my own kind, that is to say little pussies. These little pussies will proliferate rapidly and dog Trump wherever he goes. I watched *Star Trek* when your television waves reached my planet. The 'Trouble with Tribbles' episode was my favorite. Captain Kirk's trouble will pale in the face of Trump drowning in a pussy plentitude."

"I'll show you American carnage," Trump responded. "I won't be cowed by a bunch of pussies. I'll shoot all the god damn pussies."

"Won't work," said Pussy Galore. "My species is impervious to bullets."

"Then I'll lasso them with my oversized red tie."

"Nope. Won't work either. You can't lasso a pussy plethora."

True to the alien's threat, Trump was relentlessly pursued by a passel of pussies to the extent that he had to be locked up within a translucent hermetically sealed pussy proof box. When he tweeted from inside the box, he exaggeratedly the size of the pussy crowd which had gathered.

Pussy crowd size, however, was not Trump's most pressing problem. The end of his oversize tie had gotten caught in the box's closing mechanism causing him to be stuck in an uncomfortable position. Sondra felt sorry for Trump.

"Although I do not want to be part of any group which includes Trump as a member, the fact—the real fact, not the alternative fact and I know that this is stretching the definition of the word human—is that Trump is human. He should merely be contained, not tortured," Sondra said to Pussy Galore.

"Point well taken. In order to find a corrective, I must know the exact nature of the long object which is hanging from Trump's neck and constraining him. Sorry for my ignorance. Please understand that I have studied the biology of Earth women, not men. Is the object in question Trump's genitalia?"

"Yes. Yes, it's my penis. I have the biggest penis on Earth," shouted Trump from inside the box.

"Trump's lying," said Sondra. "The long red object is not Trump's genitalia. It's his tie, a garment."

"I see," intoned Pussy Galore. "In order to remove the tie from the box's closing mechanism, you need to provide its equivalent. The box will open only if you wave a tie over the box which is the exact length as the one encumbering Trump."

"No can do," said Sondra. "There's no other tie on Earth which is as unfashionably long as Trump's tie."

"Then Trump will just have to spend the rest of his life kneeling in the box."

"I have an idea. When *New York Times* columnist and Nobel Prize winning economist Paul Krugman spoke at the

Metropolitan University of New York Graduate Center on February 21, 2017, he spoofed the president by wearing a replica of his red tie. The tie almost reached Krugman's knees."

"You must bring me Krugman's tie."

Sondra phoned Krugman and explained that a ten foot tall female extraterrestrial who was the spitting image of the Pink Panther had sealed Trump in a box in a scrunched position. In order to open the box and allow Trump to get himself up, the alien needed a replica of his red tie. Krugman, thinking that nothing could be more ludicrous than the fact that Donald J. Trump was the president of the United States, agreed to cooperate. Sondra met Krugman in his office to obtain his Trump tie clone. She gave the tie to Pussy Galore who proceeded to wave it over the box. Trump was now able to stand up.

Pussy Galore, gratified that Trump would no longer be free to grab pussies, returned to her home planet.

Sondra took Krugman's tie to her office and saved it as a souvenir. Trump was kept on display to serve as a warning to Mike Pence.

Springtime for Trump

or

Feminist Extraterrestrials Eventually Produce a Woman President

Professors Maxine Bialystock and Leah Bloom were conversing in the American Studies Department lounge. There was nothing special about the circumstance—except that these faculty members where humanoid denizens of the feminist separatist planet Fallopian.

"I'm impatient," said Leah. "We've spent our careers studying America and we have nothing to show for our efforts. Enough already with the theory. I want to engage in praxis. I'm tired of being a drudge who produces scholarly texts the average Fallopian doesn't read. I want excitement. I want to be a producer."

"What would you like to produce?" asked Maxine.

"A female American president."

"Your objective is complicated."

"We're technologically awesome feminist extraterrestrials. American cultural recalcitrance won't stand a chance in the face of our powers and abilities. We can do it."

"How?"

"We can produce a male presidential candidate flop— the worst candidate on Earth who cannot fail to fail. We will arrange for him to run against a woman who is the most qualified person to be president in American history."

"Okay, I'm in. We can use our trusty android implantation within Earthlings method."

"We're seeing eye to eye. What years are we going for to undertake the implantation?"

"1946 and 1947. Now that we have a time, we need to pick a place. I suggest major metropolitan areas."

"How about suburban Chicago for the woman and outer borough New York City for the man?"

"You're on."

And so it came to pass that Dorothy Rodham and Mary Anne Trump found crystal goblets on their dining room tables. "Drink me," said the goblets to the women. They found the liquid to be delicious to the extent that they drank every drop. Hence, the androids who would be called Hillary and Donald were implanted within their Earthling host mothers' wombs.

Bialystok and Bloom used the most sophisticated Fallopian technology to program the androids. As time passed, the extraterrestrials were certain that they could not fail to produce a female American president. No one on Earth was more wonkish, competent, politically savvy, and intrepid than Hillary. No one on Earth was more narcissistic, barbaric, and prevaricating than Donald.

The Fallopians were ecstatic as they observed Hillary acting presidential in the face of Donald flinging invective and fostering hate. And when it came to pass that Donald boasted about grabbing pussies, the aliens were over the moon with confidence that no presidential candidate could be worse than him.

They were certain that they had produced a flop when they watched one of Donald's political rallies. His appearance on stage was backgrounded by a Broadway production number in which male neo-Nazis brandishing hunting rifles and lit tiki torches goose stepped while chorus line kicking eastern European super models glad in G-strings and pasties surrounded them. Everyone on stage sang "springtime for Donald and America; winter for Hillary and liberals, lock them up in a refrigerator."

"Oy. We went too far with Donald; we created a monster. I say we manipulate the election to make sure

Hillary wins," suggested Leah.

"I think we've done enough violation of the Prime Directive against interplanetary interference. In other words, at this point, we should mind our own business and stop acting like yentas. Americans invented airplanes, cars, and phones. Most importantly, they elected Obama—the greatest contemporary president in the universe. Even though their technology is primitive, Americans are not stupid," responded Maxine.

When the Fallopians continued to look at Donald's antics their viewing screens, they saw mainstream media reporters who were shocked to the extent that they fainted and were carried out on stretchers. Liberals' heads exploded. Then the aliens heard one Trump rally audience member shout "Make America Great Again." Other people joined in until the chanting reached a crescendo. Donald was a hit. Bialystock and Bloom had created President Donald J. Trump.

With the hope that Fallopian feminist technology would ultimately prevail, Bialystock and Blume went back to the drawing board. All was not lost. Dorothy Rodham and Mary Anne Trump had given birth to androids. Donald, had an "off" switch located under his orange hair. Hillary lacked this switch. Hillary was immortal. Hillary had world enough and time to be elected president—infinite springtime.

The Virginia Tech Duck Pond Engenders Stephen K. Bannon's Swamp Thing

Once upon a time in the early 1970's, Virginia Tech undergraduate Stephen K. Bannon was sauntering across the Drillfield en route to his medieval literature class in Williams Hall. The "Drillfield," the Blacksburg campus' oblong focal point, is in fact a military parade ground. Cadets, attired in grey uniforms, carry rifles and march in formation there. As the cadets goose stepped in front of him, young Stephen was recalling his recent Halloween party revelry. He had attended an on-campus gathering where his fellow students dressed as Nazi storm troopers and Jewish concentration camp victims.

The cadets' military training helped them to play their storm trooper parts well. Because the Tech campus was virtually *judenfrei,* the revelers dressed in striped pajamas and sporting magic marker placed inner wrist tattoos had to use their imaginations to enact their Halloween roles.

Since Stephen had time to kill before his class started, he crossed the road adjacent to the Drillfield and walked to the Tech Duck Pond. He sat on a bench, he threw bread to the hungry mallards, and took in the fall foliage. Suddenly he saw a brown hand brandishing a sword appear in the middle of the pond. As the ducks scattered, it became apparent that the brown handed sword carrier was a female wearing a hijab.

"Who are you?" Stephen asked. "Virginia Tech is a homogenous campus. Everyone I know here is a white Christian. What is a brown skinned alien doing in the middle of the water?"

"I am the Lady of the Duck Pond."

"My medieval lit professor, Hilbert Hillhorror, taught us about Arthurian legend and the Lady of the Lake. Professor Hillhorror stressed that the Lady of the Lake is white and blonde."

"Professor Hillhorror needs to expand his horizons. Multicultural literature is on the cusp of being in vogue. There is no reason why the Lady of the Duck Pond can't be a Muslim of color. I am she."

"This is wrong. This is a lily white campus. I want to keep it that way. Be gone from Tech's white Christian military hegemony. If you do not disappear and go back to where you came from immediately if not sooner, I will call the campus police and have them deport you. Blacksburg has no blacks. And, as the name of the Montgomery County seat 'Christiansburg' proclaims, this place is meant for white Christians. Too bad that it is not yet winter and you can't be done in by ice. It's time for me to go to Hillhorror's class where I can learn about the proper Lady of the Lake."

"Not so fast. I have arisen from the Duck Pond's depths to deliver a prophecy."

"Which is?"

"You will use a future invention called the Internet to spread hate. You will temporarily become the de facto president of the United States. You will use your experience at Virginia Tech as a model to re-engineer America. You will use your influence to negate progressive social advances and try to change America into a white Christian militaristic patriarchy."

Stephen never recovered from seeing a Muslim woman emerge from the Duck Pond depths. He spent his career perpetrating the bucolic white patriarchal milieu Tech epitomized during the 1970's.

***

Years after Stephen graduated, the Virginia Tech campus was the scene of a massacre which, at the time, was the deadliest mass shooting carried out by a single person in

American history. The massacre, perpetrated by a Tech student born in South Korea, led to intense debate about gun laws and gun violence.

When looking for evidence pertaining to the mass shooting, officials ordered that it was necessary to drain the Duck Pond. They found a skeleton lying in the muck next to a sword. A pierced rib made it obvious that the sword had been used as a murder weapon. After hearing about what had happened at his alma mater, the adult Stephen was more convinced than ever that multiculturalism had no place at Virginia Tech in general and America in particular.

The drained Duck Pond became the inception of Trump's Bannon-authored clarion call to "drain the swamp."

Marleen S. Barr

'It Is Enough If You Speak . . .
Speak Now' Talking Heads

or

Trump Rushes More To Become Unbound

I am eager to find out what happens at this interface between your American political reality and my speaking and the speaking of the ancient dramatists whom I use as a trail, as trail marks so I can move forward. My speaking exposes the dependence on reality, your reality in this instance which is not mine of which I actually comprehend very little. I only write what I imagine and this match I can't even imagine any more. . . . It is enough if you speak. Speak now. It is your play as much as it is mine. - Elfriede Jelinek, "Elfriede Jelinek's 'On the Royal Road: The Burgher King,' World Premiere Reading," *YouTube*, March 29, 2017, https://www.youtube.com/watch?v=6tZZtC2UdWI

Then there was Miss Piggy, peering down at the audience through bloody eyes, sometimes addressed or invoked by [Masha] Dakić's character throughout the show [the world premiere reading of Jelinek's 'On the Royal Road: The Burgher King,' City University of New York Graduate Center, March 27, 2017].
'Her [Miss Piggy's] hair is strange like Trump's,' noted audience member Marleen Barr. [Barr continued:] 'When Jelinek uses Miss Piggy, is she equating him with Trump? . . . Trump hates more than anything to be

laughed at. Is this like ludicrous Schwein-time for Trump?'

'I think you [Barr] got Elfriede,' [Jelinek's English translator Gitta] Honegger replied with a smile. 'She always talks about [wanting] to make the big small - to cut it down. Then she elevates Trump to Oedipus, but that then makes him all the smaller. She even confessed . . . that she put herself into Miss Piggy, too. . . . She's talking from the pedestal of the artist. She's very conscious of that.' - Shant Shahrigan, "Miss Piggy Takes Down Trump in Elfriede Jelinek's New Play," *Deutsche Welle,* March 28, 2017, http://www.dw.com/en/miss-piggy-takes-down-trump-in-elfriede-jelineks-new-play/a-38153354

Abraham Lincoln's head was the first head to realize that it could speak. Its first words were "he is not of our ilk." Lincoln's head continued: "He is not one of us. He besmirches the office we hold by having the audacity to stand with us. I say this even though I cannot stand. That fact aside, I cannot stand him. They didn't have enough money to give me a body. I'm only a head. At least I have the requisite body part to speak now. I have a mouth and I must scream about him. I have been perched up here for more than four score and seven years. I suppose that I have never spoken because I did not have anything to say. He has changed that. He is destructive to the extent that the nation may not long endure."

The head located directly next to Lincoln's head realized that it could speak too. "Speak up," said George Washington's head. "I can't turn my head. I am having difficulty hearing you."

"He is on the verge of dividing the nation to the extent that we can become engaged in a great civil war, testing whether that nation, or any nation so conceived and so dedicated, can long endure."

"I agree. I cannot tell a lie. Every word that comes out

of his mouth is a lie—including 'and' and 'the.' 'He even lies about his own name' [Jelinek]. I merely chopped down a cherry tree. His assault on the environment might eliminate cherry trees."

The Theodore Roosevelt head chimed in while moving its jaw in the manner of a rusted robot. "I am used to having a bully pulpit. He is a big bully."

The Jefferson head, hearing his fellow presidential heads, knew that it could speak too. "'Buildings are his life' [Jelinek]. I too can relate to buildings. I put great effort into constructing Monticello. I did not put a sign which reads 'Jefferson' on my home's façade. I did not name Monticello 'Jefferson Mansion.' Why were those people marching with lit torches in Charlottesville? What does 'neo-Nazi' mean?"

"I want to lead a revolutionary war against him," said the Washington head. "We all agree that he is a narcissistic vulgarian. But what can we do? We are stuck up here. No matter how much we put our heads together, we are fated to be all talk and no action. We don't even have hands—small hands or otherwise. We can't write executive orders."

The heads' eyes suddenly looked up. They saw a large silver disk in the sky moving toward them. The flying saucer landed on Washington's head. The hatch opened. A woman wearing a gold jumpsuit and gold thigh high boots emerged. She promenaded across the four presidential talking heads by flying over the gaps between them.

"Who are you and why are you walking on top of me?" asked the Roosevelt head.

"I am Jyra, a denizen of the feminist planet Menopause. Menopausians knew that he would be excruciating to the extent that you would be compelled to speak about him. Your words are relevant because 'the past is here' [Jelinek]. I am here to enable you to do more than speak. I can make it possible for you to turn your theories into praxis. You are heads. You can use your heads to do him in."

"How?" asked the Lincoln head. "We are immobile head statues."

"Yes you can."

"Yes we can?"

"Yes. All you have to do is think lovely presidential thoughts."

"Adventure," shouted Roosevelt's head.

"Victory," effused Washington's head.

"Union," insisted Lincoln's head.

"Independence," exclaimed Jefferson's head.

"Think lovelier presidential thoughts," suggested Jyra.

"Truth, justice, and the American way," chanted the heads in unison as they said the appropriate magic words, broke free of the mountain, and floated above Jyra's flying saucer. "We're liberated at last," continued the heads.

"Come into my spaceship," said Jyra as the heads followed her.

The spaceship landed on the White House lawn. The hatch opened. Jyra walked down the gangplank followed by four floating heads.

"Take me to your leader," said Jyra when a Secret Service agent approached the group.

Trump walked out of the White House and faced Jyra and the heads.

"You're a definite ten," he said to Jyra. "I want to grab your pussy."

"Not a good idea," answered Jyra. "I have powers and abilities far beyond the range of Earthling men."

"What's with the stone heads?" Trump asked. "They look sort of familiar. Oh yeah. They're former presidents. But now I'm the president and they're not. I have small hands. But they don't have any hands. No other part of me is small. None of them have one of those either."

The heads floated over to Trump and pinned him down by each positioning itself on one of his appendages.

"Since humans have two arms and two legs, four heads are better than one if the objective is to bind up said human," mused Jyra as she placed her golden boot on Trump's forehead. "The heads think that you are an embarrassment to American presidential history."

"They're just a bunch of rock heads. Rock head Roosevelt and the rest of ya, when I'm done you'll end up as a part of the great beautiful wall I will build and Mexico will pay for," Trump threatened.

"Oh you'll build all right. But it won't be a wall," fumed Jyra. "I will force you to become a new Prometheus."

"Who? Promo? I'm a master promoter," Trump declared.

"I am the master here," Jyra stated. "Heads, release Trump and float back into the ship. Trump, it will behoove you to follow behind them and get your fat ass into the ship too."

When the spaceship landed at Mount Rushmore, the heads assumed their places on the mountain. Trump stood face to face with Jyra on top of Washington's head.

"I get it," snarled Trump. "Where's the sculptor? He needs to get my likeness just right. A huge Trump head belongs on Mount Rushmore. I'm the greatest president ever. I belong up here."

"Agreed. You will be here for quite a long time. I mean flesh and blood you, not your sculpted head. When you thought that you would become a monument component, you got ahead of yourself. You will create a head which does not at all resemble your head. 'Please take your place at the sacrificial rock'" [Jelinek], said Jyra.

"No," screamed Trump.

"Resistance is futile," said the heads.

"We sound like a Greek play chorus," stated Jefferson's head.

"Appropriately so," explained Jyra. "Trump, you are about to become a Greek tragedy protagonist. You will be bound to one of the mountain's rocks. You will be all tied up. Your small hands—not your small whatever—will be your only mobile part. You will not be able to escape listening to Washington, Jefferson, Lincoln, and Roosevelt incessantly explaining what being president of the United States means. You will sculpt the head of a president who, unlike you, does not denigrate the office. You miscast Obama as not being born in the United States. Now you will literally cast him correctly. Your task is to sculpt Barack Hussein Obama's head on Mount Rushmore next to Washington's head. You love to build. So build Obama's head. Since you merely put your name on buildings and you have no artistic talent, I will magically imbue you with the ability to sculpt. You can put your name on Mount Rushmore by signing 'Trump Dummkopf' under your Obama head. If you attempt to rest, South Dakotan birds—who I hear tell are attracted to orange hair—will peck your head. When you finish Obama's head, you will be unbound and returned to Trump Tower. It will behoove you to hurry up. Elfriede Jelinek, the Nobel Prize winner from Austria, the country of Hitler's birth, equates you with Tiresias. Athena blinded Tiresias because he saw her when she was bathing. Think of all the beauty pageant contestants you ogled. In conjunction with Jelinek's Greek reference, because you bellowed 'you're fired' on reality television, I am turning you into a Promethean figure. Jelinek is right on target when she positions you in terms of Miss Piggy. You are a piggish narcissist of Miss Piggy's ilk. Even though I know more about Earth literary culture than you do—which is not hard—I am no literary critic. It takes no deep structure analysis to observe that you are a pig. Bill Maher calls you a 'whiny little bitch.' I join with Jelinek to equate you with a female pig instead of a female dog. Jelinek responds to you in terms of Mel Brooks' hilarious artistic depiction of Hitler in 'The Producers'; she has made you into a laughing stock. You hate to be laughed at. I'm laughing out loud while singing what 'On the Royal Road: The Burgher King' audience member Marleen S. Barr called 'Schwein Time For Trump.'"

"We are laughing too," the heads chortled.

It was when Trump got the mouth finished and Obama began his lectures on constitutional law that Trump decided to jump. It didn't work because every time he did an American bald eagle of gigantic proportions, the largest bald eagle ever, would pick him up and return him to the top of the mountain.

It was this eagle who finally delivered Donald to Trump Tower immediately after he finished chiseling the final letter of his name. The crowds gathered at Mount Rushmore cheered as the eagle flew off with Trump in her talons.

Note: All Elfriede Jelinek quotations included in this story are taken from her play "On the Royal Road: The Burgher King."

The Wurst President Ever

"You have to appeal more to your base," said Stephen K. Bannon. "You're not being alt-right enough."

"What should I do?" asked Trump.

"Become a Nazi."

"What about the Kushners?"

"Ivanka is no Jew. You'll just have to sacrifice her children. View them as collateral damage because only the lunatic fringe supports you. It's more fringe or nothing."

"I have other grandchildren. I don't want to be a loser. Nazism here I come."

"*Heil* Trump," said Bannon with right arm raised.

"*Heil* myself," Trump proclaimed.

Bannon cut off a piece of Trump's orange hair. He then used Crazy Glue to attach the hair above Trump's upper lip. "Great mustache. Remove the too big suit and put on these clothes."

Trump stood in front of Bannon wearing a brown military outfit emblazoned with swastikas and jack boots.

"You look like a Nazi. Now you have to sound like one. Let's start at the very beginning, a very good place to start. Do you know any German?"

"I only speak Queens English."

"Speaking Nazi is easy. Repeat after me—loudly. *Achtung. Raus Juden.*"

"*Achtung. Raus Juden,*" Trump screamed.

"You're ready to come down the Trump Tower escalator and start your Nazi schtick."

Trump entered the Trump Tower lobby which was emblazoned with Nazi flags. The white male audience held flaming tiki torches which they purchased from the Hawaii

Kai Restaurant. "*Heil* Trump," they shouted.

"*Achtung. Raus Juden,*" Trump vociferously answered.

A group of burly men immediately exited the lobby and smashed the clock located in front of Trump Tower. A reporter put a microphone in front of a clock destroyer's mouth.

"I don't want to see no time," the vandal explained. "Time is truth. I just wanna get rid of the Jews, the blacks, and the women. White men's lives matter," bellowed the destroyer.

Trump entered his golden Trump Tower apartment. "The mustache itches," he said to Bannon.

"You need to keep it. It's an integral part of your new Nazi persona. And another thing. Presidents have pets. You need to get a pet."

Melania entered wearing a dirndl and a woolen *Tracht* jacket. A German shepherd followed her. "The dog's name is Wulf-Adolph Trump," she said. "Remember that I Germanized my name by changing it from Knavs to Knauss. Biden's wife Jill insisted upon being called Dr. Biden. I want to be called Frau Knauss. Unlike my alternative fact Germanicness, you really are German."

"Yeah. My grandfather Frederick, originally named Friedrich, was born in Kallstadt. Dad lied and said that we were from Scandinavia. There are a lot of Jews in Queens. If the kids in the Kew-Forest School knew that I was part German, they would not have liked me.

"The Trumps responded like the British royal family," said Bannon. "The royals hid their German origins too. Those Windsors were originally named for the House of Saxe-Coburg and Gotha. Unlike them, you are openly reclaiming your rightful German heritage." Wulf-Adolf loped toward Trump and held up his paw.

"I like this pet thing," said Trump as he patted Wulf-Adolph's head. "But I want a more huge pet. Like a German draft horse, the biggest horse in the world. I want to have a draft horse named Horst."

"I'll arrange it. Meanwhile I've scheduled a rally for you

in Michigan. There are a lot of Germans there," said Bannon.

"I won't have to drink the water in Flint will I?" Trump asked. Once assured he wouldn't, he agreed to go to Michigan.

Upon arrival, Trump re-glued his orange moustache and stepped out on the swastika sodden Michigan stage. Scantily clad beauty pageant contestants carrying pretzels and beer steins performed chorus line kicks behind him. Male dancers wearing lederhosen careened across the stage.

"*Achtung. Raus Juden,*" yelled Trump. "There's free wurst for everyone. I love beautiful wurst." According to Bannon, the rally was a success.

Trump flew back to New York and pointed a thumbs up at the destroyed clock when he entered Trump Tower.

A reporter standing in the Trump Tower lobby asked Trump to justify holding a Nazi rally.

"Good people and bad people attend my rallies," Trump told the reporter. "Take the rally we held here in the Tower last week. Some good people merely wanted to remove the clock."

Trump was interrupted by someone bellowing "*achtung*" in a Brooklyn accent. "I'm Mel Brooks. I helped to liberate a concentration camp. See that guy floating up there? He's the real Hitler, not a false orange mustached alternative fact Hitler." Brooks pointed to where a giant Hitler head floated.

An authentic German accented "*achtung*" emanating from Hitler's mouth permeated the Trump Tower lobby as he began to shout orders in German.

"Let me translate," said Frau Knauss, who had just come down the escalator. "Hitler says that smashing the clock tore the space time continuum. He was able to step through the resulting hole and emerge floating above us."

Jared Kushner entered the lobby. "You victimized my grandparents," he said to Hitler.

"I regret that they escaped the ovens," Hitler answered.

"*Raus Juden,*" interjected Trump. "The space time

hole is huge. Look at all the people pouring in here."

Loud mouthed World War Two era Jewish New York women crowded the lobby and addressed Trump.

"You like beauty pageant contestants? Well I was Miss America," shouted Bess Myerson. "I dare you to try to grab my pussy."

"I'm a tough Upper West Side broad and I won't take any shit from you," screamed Lauren Bacall.

"Your mouth is not bigger than my mouth," yelled Bella Abzug as she threw her hat at Trump's head.

"You are certainly not louder than me," sang Ethel Merman. "I am not Jewish. I just came to sing my two cents in."

American World War Two military personnel arrived. They were Women's Army Corps members now serving as female ghost busters. "Hitler, go back to 1945 and become the corpse you were," demanded the WACs. "Auf Wiedersehen," said Hitler as he disappeared.

"Trump, as for you, resign now," the WACs said in unison. "A Nazi can't be president in America."

Trump complied in the wake of the WACs' successful military coup. Our female ancestors restored American democracy when they ensconced Hillary as president.

A Syrian immigrant who was selling pretzels outside Trump Tower near the remains of the smashed clock smiled when he heard the news about the new president.

Mel Brooks triumphantly sang "Springtime for Trump" at the Tony Awards. Robert De Niro responded by walking on stage and launching an F-bomb at Trump.

Trump Learns That Climate Change Does Not Impact the Phantom Zone

Part One:
Trump's Close Encounter with a Fellow Incredible Hulk

A hulking figure who resembled Darth Vader, sans helmet, strode across the White House lawn. Secret Service agents fired assault rifles when the hulk refused to halt. The heat rays which emerged from his eyes melted the bullets. "Take me to your leader," the extraterrestrial said to the agents.

Another incredible hulk who seemed too orange to be real also strode across the lawn. Intimidated by facing someone taller than James Comey, Trump extended his hand determined to win the male power handshake game he had played with French President Emmanuel Macron. If Trump failed to win the handshake duration game, he could resort to the shove aside method he effectively wielded against the Prime Minister of Montenegro.

Trump hand squeezed as hard as he could while the alien merely smirked. When the alien squeezed back, Trump careened to the ground

"Surrender," said the alien. "My powers and abilities are greater than yours."

"I've never met anyone whose powers and abilities are greater than mine," stated Trump.

"Surprise. I'm not a person. Call me General Zod. I just escaped from the Phantom Zone," explained the extraterrestrial.

"Phantom Zone? You are as powerful as Superman? How the hell did you escape?"

"It was foretold that the Zone's encasement would crack when the president of the United States grasped an orb while accompanied by a Saudi Arabian sheik and a damsel in distress. Melania qualifies to be the damsel. Although this confluence was unlikely to ensue, it did—and here I am. Join with me to take over Earth."

"Sounds good. I love strong leaders. An extraterrestrial superman is even more powerful than Putin. You've got a deal. I'm so great at making deals. I want to close this deal at Mar-a-Lago."

General Zod took Trump in his arms and flew him to Florida. Because Trump did not want to resemble Lois Lane—and he felt this way even though he had curtsied to the sheik—he attached a huge "Trump Shuttle" sign to Zod's chest.

Upon landing at Mar-a-Lago, the two sat down to dinner. "I wish that you had been around during the campaign," Trump said to Zod. "A super powered being could have influenced the election much more effectively than the Russians. Never repeat that. Have some chocolate cake. It's the best chocolate cake. It comes with vanilla ice cream. I get two scopes and you get one. Despite your super powers, that's the way it is—because I said so. I'm going to fill ya in on some huge state secrets."

News of Trump's close encounter with a Phantom Zone escapee pervaded the media. Professor Sondra Lear had an anxiety attack when she heard Trump and Zod announce their plans for world domination.

When Putin fired nuclear weapons to stop the American and the alien from usurping him, Zod pushed the weapons aside. Sondra was determined to use her scholarly expertise to save Earth. She resolved to turn her lifelong devotion to feminist science fiction theory into praxis by resorting to flying. Since, unlike Zod, she lacked the ability to fly, she booked a flight to Iowa City. Because New York was devoid of kryptonite, she intended to quash Zod by searching for Smallville in Iowa and trying to find kryptonite there. Iowa was certainly a better kryptonite hunting ground than New York.

Sondra's trip to Iowa made perfect sense. She grew up in Forest Hills, Queens, just a stone's throw away from Trump's childhood home in Jamaica Estates. Her outer borough experience put her at a distinct disadvantage vis-à-vis accomplishing her plan to nullify Zod. Since Sondra had always lived in New York's concrete jungle, she lacked small town formative experiences. According to her perspective, Briarwood, a small Queens neighborhood, was tantamount to Smallville. Briarwood would be considered huge in Iowa. Because she had taught in the University of Iowa English department, Iowa City was not terra incognito.

Sondra walked into the Iowa English department and knocked on the office door of her friend Professor Merryl Hymm. After Sondra explained her plan to Merryl, the Iowa faculty member advised Sondra to try her luck finding kryptonite in Coralville, an Iowa City bedroom community.

Sondra, with a large backpack slung over her shoulder—attired in a pith helmet and khaki suit accessorized with no gun and compass—started to search for kryptonite in Coralville. She noticed an indentation in the ground of a corn field which was devoid of corn in one spot. While poking around in the dirt, she found red, green, and gold kryptonite. She filled her backpack with the gold variety. After Merryl drove her to the airport, Sondra boarded a Palm Beach bound flight.

She showed up at the door of her distant cousin who owned beach front property near Mar-a-Lago. Although Sondra's cousin was not willing to share her wealth with Sondra, she was happy to help thwart Trump and Zod. Sondra changed into her cousin's bathing suit, put the gold kryptonite filled backpack over her shoulder, and walked into the ocean. Aware of the law which mandates that every beach in America is public property up to the high water mark, she swam over to Mar-a-Lago. Sondra emerged from the water, walked up to the high water mark, and threw the gold kryptonite on to the dry sand. Objective accomplished, she swam back to her cousin's mansion.

She looked over her shoulder while swimming and saw none other than Trump appear on his beach. Unable to resist gold rocks, he picked them up and brought them inside Mar-a-Lago.

"It seems that I am now richer than I was when I left the house a few minutes ago," Trump informed Zod. "Look at this. I found gold on the beach. Maybe it washed up from a sunken Spanish galleon. I love the Spanish."

"That's not gold," gasped Zod as he clenched his chest and careened to the floor. "I'm the only thing that is washed up. Get rid of those rocks immediately."

"Doing so is a bad deal. Do you expect me to throw away gold? I owe you nothing. I will keep the gold and throw you under a yellow bus."

The kryptonite was causing Zod to hyperventilate and become jaundiced to the extent that his skin matched Trump's hair.

"Please remove the rocks," pleaded Zod. "I'm super allergic to them. You have more to gain from conquering the world with me than from keeping the fool's gold rocks."

"Fine," muttered Trump as he returned to the beach.

When Trump threw the rocks into the ocean, he noticed a plane flying along the beach pulling a banner. Sondra wrote the following banner text and convinced her cousin to pay for it: "Zod, return to the Phantom Zone or else. This means you. There's more available gold kryptonite." As an English professor, Sondra was accustomed to authoring lengthy texts.

"I have it on good authority that if you don't return to the Phantom Zone you will closely encounter more gold rocks," said Trump to Zod.

Zod, not a fan of gold kryptonite or Trump, if the truth be known, re-entered the extraterrestrial prison and never returned to Earth. Trump, depressed because he lost his chance to achieve world domination, consoled himself with the thought that he had recovered from loss before. He had survived the Atlantic City casino bankruptcy fiasco. So too for the Zod disappearance. There were other strong dictators in the world. If necessary, Trump could strike up another deal with Putin. Putin declined and instead had Trump banished to Mar-a-Logo. Hillary was then made president by acclimation.

Part Two:
Trump's Poseidon Adventure

Trump was walking on the beach at Mar-a-Lago when he saw a bearded man holding a trident striding into the Mar-a-Lago living room.

"I'm afraid to ask, but who the hell are you?" inquired Trump.

Sondra, still staying with her cousin, knew the answer. During her return swim, she became acquainted with two dolphins who said that Poseidon wanted to do a deal with Trump. Knowing that climate change would eventually sink Mar-a-Lago, he wanted to purchase it at a huge discount and turn it into a subterranean palace. The dolphins, by holding support polls in their mouths, used a viewing screen to show Sondra what was ensuing between Trump and Poseidon.

Sondra watched Trump decline Poseidon's offer. "Climate change is a hoax. I refuse to sell Mar-a-Lago for cheap," he said.

Poseidon banged his trident against the floor three times. Water rapidly seeped into the living room. "The seas will eventually inundate your property," said Poseidon.

Sondra asked the dolphins if Poseidon had a daughter.

"Yes. Her name is Idrenchka," one dolphin answered.

"Please ask Idrenchka to speak with me." A beautiful

blonde mermaid swam up to Sondra.

"Hello Idrenchka. I hope that you are more reasonable than your patriarchal father. As fellow women, maybe we can work together."

"How can I be of help?"

"Tell your father that instead of trying to acquire cheap real estate he should convince Trump that climate change is real."

Sondra did not have much faith in this proposed collaboration. The dolphins told her that Idrenchka had led a sheltered life growing up in undersea palaces. Her professional experience was limited to selling designer coral encrusted brassieres to her fellow mermaids. Her shoe line failed for the obvious reason.

Despite her limitations, Idrenchka tried her best to do what Sondra asked. "Daddy, the humans will suffer if climate change causes their homes to float away," she said to Poseidon. "Convince Trump to sign the Paris Climate Accords."

"Even a supernatural being can't convince Trump of anything," Poseidon answered.

"I met this nice human professor who told me that water can act like something called kryptonite in relation to humans. It can kill them. Just tell Trump that you will drown him if he refuses to sign the Accords."

"Sign or drown," said Poseidon to Trump.

Trump, horrified by the threat of being water boarded by a trident carrying wet back, complied.

Sondra—with a sense of missions accomplished—got out of the ocean, changed into her cousin's clothes, went to the airport, and flew back to New York. She was proud that her good judgment enabled her to save the world twice.

Welcoming more mundane activity, she walked into her office and started to grade final exams. She put her pen down and grasped the chunk of gold kryptonite she kept on her desk to use as a paper weight. She was prepared in case one of Zod's cronies tried to do an Earth shattering deal with Trump. Sondra knew that in the age of Trump feminists had to be super heroes.

Trump Is Nothing Like the Sun

Perhaps he [Trump] felt the need to make clear that he was a force of nature decades before [Hurricane] Harvey came along. . . . 'What a crowd!' he [Trump] boomed and beamed. 'What a turnout!' All the water in the world couldn't drown his satisfaction. - Frank Bruni, "As the Waters Swell, So does Trump's Ego," New York Times, August 30, 2017, A22

"The totality refers to me. I am the focus of world media. I can't deal with people looking at the eclipse instead of looking at me. Nothing eclipses me," said Trump to Melania as they stepped out on the White House porch to view the sun and the moon doing their thing. Melania daintily donned her protective glasses. Trump lacked any such gear. Glasses-clad Melania looked up while Trump gazed skyward with naked eyes.

"Don't look. Don't look," chanted the crowd assembled beneath the porch. Trump, who never listened to anyone, acted as usual. "I'm glad that's over," he said. "Now people can resume looking at me instead of at the sun."

"I'm glad too," responded Melania. "I'm used to wearing designer sunglasses, not these cheap tacky ones."

Trump went back inside the White House and sat down to watch cable news. Just as he was about to launch a tweet storm, he saw an unidentified flying object hovering above his television screen. The object turned out to be a small pink reptilian creature with spread purple wings. She blinked her round blue eyes and stared dead on at Trump.

"What the hell are you?" barked Trump.

"I am the dragon who, according to Chinese legend, eats the sun and causes an eclipse. Because you were stupid enough to look directly at the sun during an eclipse, I materialized to check you out. Eating the sun for eternity is boring. Besides, I'm on a diet. You're the only person who can see me. I'm going to entertain myself by following you around. Consider yourself to be haunted by a Chinese fire breathing dragon."

"A dragon—Chinese, fire breathing or otherwise—is the last thing I need. I have enough trouble with Mueller breathing down my neck. I can't even use you as a photo op in case I insult Chinese immigrants. I'm not up to them yet 'cause I'm still busy bullying the Mexicans and the Muslims. My formative encounter with China happened when I was growing up in Jamaica Estates and I ate Chinese food in the Len Hing restaurant on Queens Boulevard. The dragon pictured on the front of their menu was not pink and purple like you. In honor of that menu, I'm going to name you Chop Suey, Choppy for short. Now get the hell outta here Choppy."

"I'm in charge, not you," stated Choppy.

Trump, trying to do business as usual, walked into his bedroom. Because he was horny, he phoned Melania.

"Get your ass in here now. I want sex."

Melania arrived to perform her contractual duties. Trump was sprawled on his bed with Choppy hovering above. Melania, of course, was unable to see the dragon.

"What do you want?" asked Melania.

"The usual. Get to work."

"I want five more gowns."

"Sure. Now get started."

Choppy, adjusting her fire breathing temperature to low, blew hot air over Melania's back.

"Donnie, oh Donnie oh this is the first time that you have ever made me feel hot," panted Melania.

"I'm done." Trump said and zipped up. Trump didn't give a damn about what Melania wanted. He got dressed, walked to the Oval Office, and confronted Stephen K. Bannon.

"You're fired," Trump bellowed. "Ivanka says that I hafta get rid of ya."

"What?" Bannon asked.

"I said you're fired."

Choppy set the carpet on fire.

"I get it. I'm fired. There's no reason to incinerate my feet," said Bannon as he stormed out of the White House and made his way to the Breitbart News Network office.

Choppy routinely breathed fire whenever Trump acted like Trump. The White House staff, in response to the newly routine mini conflagrations, began carrying fire extinguishers. Choppy set fire to all the Executive Orders enclosed within folders which resembled Chinese restaurant menu covers. When Choppy burned Trump's cellphone, CNN devoted multitudinous panels to trying to discern why he had suddenly gone cold tweeting turkey. Attributing the cause to a fire breathing dragon never entered the panelists' minds.

"I have a burning question," Trump said to Choppy. "How about putting your fire breathing to good use? Go and burn up the failing New York Times. Or the next time the Nazis march, light their tiki torches. Do something constructive."

"No."

"Why not?"

"I'm not on your side. You had the audacity to stare directly at the sun when I was in the middle of eating it. It is not polite to watch someone while they're eating."

"There's no such thing as dragons. Why do I hafta be bothered by you?"

"There's no such thing as the stuff which comes out of your lying mouth. Just consider me a real—that is only real to you—alternative truth."

"Are there other alternatives?"

"As a matter of fact, yes," said a gorgeous young man wearing a white toga. He was standing in a chariot which had a horse attached to it. Several horses usually pulled the chariot. A temporary austerity budget on Mount Olympus caused him to cut back on transportation costs.

"I was just getting used to the pesty dragon and now I have to deal with you and your horse. You look gay. Don't even think about marrying me. My base does not approve of gay marriage. All the horse shit comin' outa here comes from me. I create quite enough horse shit, thank you very much. By the way, who the hell are you?" said Trump.

"Apollo. When you looked directly at the sun, you brought me here too. Unlike Choppy, I am visible to everyone."

"Then put on appropriate clothes. You look like you're wearin' a sheet. Although the recently fired Bannon would say otherwise, perhaps I should not be seen fraternizing with a sheet wearer. Choppy, what should I do about the horse?"

"Figure it out."

Trump mounted up and trotted out to the White House lawn. Reporters gathered as he struck a rigid and serious pose.

"I'm solving the politically incorrect monument problem," Trump explained to the reporters. "My base is angry about removing Robert E. Lee and Stonewall Jackson statues. De Blasio is thinking about taking Columbus out of Columbus Circle. Who's next? Washington and Jefferson? What's with the dead white guy statues when you can monumentalize flesh and blood moi?"

Trump began routinely to sit on the horse and pose as a monument. The horse ate some White House lawn grass and hence, lowered the lawn mowing bill. Meanwhile, Choppy was still being incendiary. Although Trump satisfied his ego by attributing Melania's new sexual flushes to his sexual prowess, he was not happy. He was tired of having his papers and phones burned. He was also losing patience with the effort to hoist his corpulence on to the horse. Trump wished that he was not saddled with Choppy and Apollo. When exhaustion caused him to try to take a nap, he looked up and saw a white haired man wearing a white antiquate suit floating above him.

"Quite a lot of whiteness here. Your suit is an improvement over the toga. I'm afraid to ask but who the hell are you?" questioned Trump.

'The name is Twain, Mark Twain."

"Oh yeah. They taught me about ya in the Kew-Forest School. I remember some book about a prince and a pauper. The pauper is a loser. I wanted to be the prince. What are ya doin' here?"

"I'm taking a break from writing about an eclipse in order to meet a New York Yankee who tries to thwart America's courts."

"Enough already. How do I get rid of you, Choppy, and Apollo?"

"Wait for the next eclipse. Eclipses happen all the time. Go to one and look at it with protective glasses. When you do, we will all disappear. Choppy will go back to eating the sun. Apollo and the horse will go back to driving the sun across the sky. I'll go back to writing about an eclipse's impact." Trump, as usual, refused to listen.

It started to rain. Rain was general all over Houston. Trump traveled there to do a Hurricane Harvey photo op. Melania, with designer raincoat in hand, boarded Air Force One with Trump. Harvey usurped her need for designer sunglasses.

When Trump exited the plane and faced the crowd, he praised the first responders and congratulated himself on the huge crowd size. He was totally blind to the plight of the flood victims, though. Choppy, Apollo, the horse, and Twain knew that his blindness had nothing to do with viewing the eclipse sans protective eyewear. Trump would not allow the sun and the rain to eclipse his ego.

Choppy, who unlike Trump was able to see beyond herself, felt sorry for the flood victims. Helping them would give her the opportunity to unleash her huge full fire breathing capacity. While located inside the White House, she had merely wanted to irk Trump—not cause a War of 1812 style White House public burning. She would not have that problem while hovering in the open air above Houston's flood zones. She flew there and upon arrival raised her flame heat level to high. The heat caused the flood waters to evaporate. Apollo did his part by driving the sun across Houston. Twain gave a reading from *A Connecticut Yankee in King Arthur's Court* at the storm's next stop, the Mississippi Valley, raising money for the flood victims.

Trump continued to refuse to be eclipsed. Realizing that he, unlike most presidents, lacked a pet—an invisible dragon did not count as a pet—he enlisted the horse to serve in that capacity. Soon all the papers were taking pictures of the rear of the horse and using Trump's name in the caption. Such is how it came to pass that this was the model for Trump's official portrait after his departure from the White House. Nobody complained, even though the painting's title is "A Horse's Ass."

Trump's Tweets are Really for the Birds

There are already countless birders in the city. . . .
They witness lyrical clouds of songbirds in the spring
migration. Predatory hawks supply now routine
melodrama. . . . 'Never give up listening to the sounds
of birds' was his [Audubon's] advice. - Francis X.
Clines, "Take the A Train, as in Audubon," *New York*
Times, May 8, 2017

It all started when Bambi Bamberg-Lipschitz left her window open. This event would have been unremarkable except for the fact that Bambi lived in Manhattan. Manhattan denizens, to avoid soot sodden apartments, hardly ever open windows. This penchant applied to Bambi even though she lived in a Trump Tower condo and, of course, had a maid. Polly Bamberg-Lipschitz took it upon herself to exit the condo via the open window.

Polly was not a suicidal psychopath who intended to jump to her Fifth Avenue pavement splattered death. Polly, completely unscathed, flew toward Central Park. Her ability to fly was unremarkable; Polly is a parrot. She was merely sick of being cooped up in Bambi's condo. She was now relishing her freedom to fly around Central Park and perch in trees. But Polly was not happy. The park was devoid of parrots. Polly longed to flock with her own kind. So she lit out for the outer borough territories.

Having heard Bambi say that Brooklyn was becoming more desirable than Manhattan, Polly headed there. She discerned squawks emanating from Brooklyn College's main gate. Upon arrival, Polly found a thriving monk parrot colony descended from Kennedy Airport pet shipment escapees. These parrots had successfully become Brooklynites. When Polly voiced her intention to join her fellows, she was warmly welcomed as a new flock member.

Individual parrots are able to teach human language to other parrots. The wild parrots were not up on the latest political discourse. Polly, in contrast, was a captive audience when Bambi, a fervent liberal Democratic feminist, railed against Trump every hour on the hour. Bambi incessantly repeated utterances such as "the orange outrage pussy grabber is not my president." Polly mimicked all of Bambi's expressions of outrage against her obnoxious neighbor who had become the president of the United States.

While welcoming Polly, one of the wild parrots articulated a normal parrot locution. "Polly want a cracker?" she asked. Jeff Sessions materialized in front of the Brooklyn College gate. Students prevented him from entering the campus and ordered him to return to the Alabama plantation he came from.

Polly tried her best to fit into the flock. She had arrived during nest building season. While everyone was fashioning twigs into circular structures, Polly's architectural purview emanated from Bambi's latest fashion accessory. Instead of gathering twigs, Polly headed toward the pink wool protruding from a yarn store's curbside garbage bag. She wove the yarn into a pussy hat which exactly resembled the one Bambi proudly wore. Polly triumphantly attached her creation to a tree branch and sat down within it.

It did not take Polly long to teach the flock to mimic Bambi. The Brooklyn College community became accustomed to hearing the parrots screech "orange outrage," "pussy grabber," and "small hands." Sparrows and robins got wind of what the parrots were saying. Wanting to be part of the action, they joined in. Soon all the campus birds—starlings and pigeons included—were flying around expositing anti-Trump rhetoric. The cackle did not remain confined to the campus. Green-Wood Cemetery monk parrots soon contributed to the din. Their feathered friends in Central, Prospect, and Pelham Bay Parks—and even in Staten Island's Clove Lakes Park—joined them. The entire Jamaica Bay Wildlife Refuge avian population emitted a cacophony of anti-Trump commentary. Even the descendants of Pale Male the red-tailed hawk said that they coveted "huge" and "bigly" rats for supper.

Polly was interviewed on CNN and MSNBC. Sitting on stage with a little pink pussy hat perched on her green head, she explained to Anderson Cooper and Rachel Maddow that she was speaking her mind. She agreed with Bambi's antipathy toward Trump.

And so it came to pass that Trump heard that all the birds in New York were parroting back every asinine and racist thing he said. Trump knew exactly how he would counter the bird verbiage. He engaged in a predawn tweet storm. "The birds are for the birds. Birds can't tweet better than me. Not," Trump tweeted.

The Brooklyn College parrots, reading Trump's tweets on the phones they kept in their nests, were outraged that Trump alleged that he could tweet better than they could tweet. They turned to Polly to advise them how to react. Polly based her response on Bambi's description of the Women's March on Washington. She spread the word through the bird grapevine that all New York birds should flock to Trump Tower when Trump was next in residence.

As Trump's limousine emerged from the Lincoln Tunnel and proceeded across 34th Street, he looked up and saw the sky sodden with circling seagulls. Fifth Avenue was crowded with pigeons to the extent that he could hardly access the Trump Tower lobby. As Trump tried to enter the building, crows pecked at his orange haired head and red-tailed hawks dropped rats on him.

Polly flew into the lobby with a parrot-sized bullhorn attached to her leg. "Attention. Attention. All humans in Trump Tower, with the exception of Trump, evacuate immediately if not sooner," she loudly squawked. When the humans saw the sun eclipsed by a hovering bird plethora, they did as they were told. Tourists, building workers, and multimillion dollar condo owners filed out while covering their heads. Trump was the only "human" who remained in Trump Tower.

Polly stood at the helm of the amassed avian army. "On the count of three, let loose," she said into the bullhorn as she began to count down. When the birds heard "three," they simultaneously dropped droppings. The dried droppings formed a crust on Trump Tower's façade; it took months to remove. Trump was as imprisoned in Trump Tower as Polly had been. The birds had transformed the building into a Trump cage. Caged bird Trump was not singing.

Bambi, locked out of her condo, was temporarily homeless. Using her situation as an opportunity to change her materialistic purview, she matriculated at Brooklyn College as a women's studies major and moved into a dorm. The socialite became a bird lady who daily fed the parrots canapés, sushi, and arugula.

During her daily parrot food dispersal, Bambi consulted with Polly about the best way to resist Trump. Polly loved to converse while perched on the ear of Bambi's pussy hat.

Trump, meanwhile, had time to contemplate the implications of being in deep tweet-induced bird shit. Until Trump Tower was cleaned, he had nothing to do but sit inside and tweet. But because everyone was reading Polly's Twitter feed, Trump no longer had any social media followers.

Terminating Trump's Biting Remarks

Americans should have known. All the signs were there. The small mouth hides his fangs. The comments about Megyn Kelly's "whatever" and Mika Brzezinski's face were symptomatic of his obsession with blood. Perhaps he invited Mika to Mar-a-Lago because he craved a midnight snack. Some people call him a fake president, but Trump is a real vampire.

When Mika mocked him, he felt betrayed by someone who, like him, descended from Eastern Europeans. Due to his ties to his ancestral home in Transylvania, he married two women who grew up in proximity to that locale. He divorced them because he had a yen for fresh blood. His fondness for Putin is more about locational nostalgia than political affinity. Who knew that Bill Cosby drugged those women to provide Trump with more bodies to sink his teeth into? The beauty pageant contestants never realized that grabbing pussies was not Trump's primary objective. He wanted to suck their blood. When the beauty queens amassed around The Donald, they were unaware that the "D" in his name most importantly referred to "Dracula."

Trump became a real estate developer in order to build an appropriate vampire abode on Fifth Avenue. True, Trump Tower is no bat infested foreboding castle. But the imposing dark building surrounded by pigeons is as spooky as midtown Manhattan architecture gets.

Yes, being elected president made Trump the most powerful man on Earth. But he was in it for the blood. Think of all the people who will die if he successfully repeals Obama Care. The more people die, the more available blood Trump will have to ingest. If health care repeal fails, Trump can always resort to using the nuclear codes. Nuclear war would provide Trump with more food than open access to all the all you can eat buffets in America.

What does it mean that the fake president is a real vampire? Trump is sucking the life's blood out of American social progress. Women were becoming more empowered. Minorities were enjoying improving opportunities. Now women live in fear of being treated like protagonists in *The Handmaid's Tale*. Black football stars are designated as "sons of bitches."

Professor Sondra Lear embarked upon a plan to use food to do Trump-the-vampire in. She was initially glad to note that President Trump was progressively getting fatter. His weight gain could be attributed to caloric intake from normal food as well as from blood. Trump, after all, rhapsodized about the best chocolate cake in the world and demanded two scoops of vanilla ice cream when everyone else received one. Sondra soon realized that garden variety food would not serve as Trump's Waterloo. Although Trump's panty line was visible when his huge derrière was pictured in white tennis shorts, his presidency continued. Trump's suits and the damage he inflicted continued to expand.

It occurred to Sondra that nutritional deprivation, not overeating, was the key to ending Trump's presidency. She enacted her plan by writing an article for the *New York Times* which provided scholarly evidence derived from analyzing horror fiction to reveal that Trump is a vampire. In a subsequent *Times* article, she stated that if the vampire president was deprived of blood, he would become too weak to stay in office. Her point: if Trump became isolated from all people—and, hence, all blood-filled bodies—he would be unable to ingest his major nutritional source. This procedure was easy to implement. Nobody on Earth really wanted to be near Trump.

People took Sondra's advice. Trump found himself alone in the White House. With his blood food source cut off, Trump became weaker and weaker. He was incapacitated to the extent that he was unable to tweet. Sondra's science fiction expertise enabled America to be saved by a bloodless revolution.

Trump Uses 'The Local Milk People' to Lure Pussies Out of the White House Basement

I hate taking these people. I guarantee you they are bad. That is why they are in prison right now. They are not going to be wonderful people who go on to work for the local milk people. - Donald Trump, *Twitter,* August 3, 2017

"Your approval ratings are tanking. You need to act more like other presidents," Kellyanne Conway told Trump.

"I can at once own gold-plated toilets and convince uneducated working class people that I am one of them," Trump snapped. "Other presidents couldn't do that."

"I'm just asking you to stop acting like an animal and get an animal. Roosevelt's Scottish Terrier Fala is buried with him. Johnson's Little Beagle Johnson was called 'LBJ' too. Get with the presidential pet program," said Kellyanne as she removed two kittens from her statement bag.

"They can stay. I'll name them Marla and Ivana after the pussies I rehomed because they bored me. The names will put those bitches in their place."

Ivana and Marla, like their human namesakes and most sane people, despised Trump. The moment he stopped grabbing them, they hightailed it out of the Oval Office. They headed to the White House basement where they survived on mice and kitchen garbage. Trump did not give the pussies further thought.

It never occurred to him that he should have named Ivana Ivan. When the White House staff confronted a basement swarming with pussies, they recognized that Trump's pussy problem was analogous to Captain Kirk's trouble with tribbles.

"Like the human Marla and Ivana, the pussies had the greatest sex ever," said Trump to Kellyanne when he was informed of the overpopulation problem. "I got rid of two wives. Now I will do the same with the pussies galore. I'll hit 'em with fire and fury like the world has never seen."

A bespectacled male figure with off center parted hair floated into the Oval Office. "Threatening cats with power greater than the bombing of Hiroshima is a little much," the figure said. "You have no right to change Washington into a wasteland."

"Who the hell are you?" bellowed Trump. "I have to contend with a basement filled with pesty pussies. I don't have time for you."

"There will be time, there will be time to prepare a face to meet the faces that you meet."

"Are you some kind of veterinarian?"

"No, you vulgarian. I am most certainly not a veterinarian. I wrote *Old Possum's Book of Practical Cats*. It was turned into a Broadway play which did not bomb. You have no right to threaten to bomb cats. I am T. S. Eliot."

"Neva heard of ya."

"Let's not be narrow, nasty, and negative," said Eliot as he disappeared in a smoke puff huff.

"Eliot is right. You can't bomb cats," said Kellyanne. "Cats love milk. We can hire the local milk people to supply a lot of milk. They can put the milk in the Rose Garden. All the cats will march out of the basement to drink the milk."

Satisfied that he had solved the pussy problem, Trump glanced out of an Oval Office window. He had a cow when he saw a flying cow. More specifically, he saw a spaceship which looked like a cow. The bovine look-a-like spaceship landed on the White House lawn. The hatch opened. A group of breasts came bouncing out.

Eliot re-materialized. "You never heard of me. How about Philip Roth? Have you heard of him?"

"Nope."

"He wrote *The Breast*, a text about a personified breast becoming real. You are obviously closely encountering extraterrestrials who adhere to Roth's vision."

"First I had pussies in the basement and now there's tits on the lawn. At least they're big tits. They're bigger than Melania's tits and that's saying something because her tits are huge. I rate the extraterrestrial tits as a ten."

"Humankind cannot bear very much reality," said Eliot as he did another smoke puff huff disappearing act.

The biggest breast stepped forward when Trump emerged from the White House. "Take me to your leader," she said.

"I'm the leader because I beat crooked Hillary. I had the greatest Electoral College victory in history. My Inauguration Day crowd was bigger than Obama's. Who the hell are you? And normally I only grope pussies, but I'd really like to grope you too."

"We come from the feminist planet Mammary. You referred to the local milk people. From our perspective, we are the local milk people. How can we be of service?"

"I need to get rid of pussies. I want to go down a notch from resorting to fire and fury and use milk."

"No problem. We've got milk."

"A group of breasts emerged from the spaceship and floated above Trump. Streams of milk cascaded from their nipples and splattered over Trump's head. His orange hair took on a white hew. As he licked the milk off of his lips, Trump thought about the golden shower he experienced in Russia. The milk—no skim milk here—was out of this world super fat sodden extraterrestrial milk. Ingesting it proved to be the straw that broke the camel's back vis-à-vis Trump's huge cholesterol level. He had a heart attack. As the news of his hospitalization broke, people were grateful that Trump was now unable to start a nuclear war over a pussy plethora to divert attention from Mueller's investigation.

Eliot reappeared followed by the cats attracted to the smell of the milk soaked White House lawn. They lapped up the milk and sang: "Memory/ All alone in the moonlight/ I can smile at the old days/ I was beautiful then/ I remember the time I knew what happiness was / Let the memory live again" ["Memory," *Cats*, Lyrics by T. S. Eliot and Trevor Nunn]. They could sing because they were no ordinary pussies; they were personified *Cats* cats.

Marla the pussy ran for president. There was, after all, no law against a singing cat's candidacy. Because the electorate was fed up with both the Democrats and the Republicans—that is to say all human presidential candidates—she won a landslide victory.

Trump never imagined that a pussy would be the first female president—and his successor. Marla successfully nullified every aspect of Trump's presidency.

Their mission to Earth accomplished, the local milk people blasted off to return to Mammary. For the benefit of Mammarian literature students, they welcomed Eliot aboard. With a nod toward all of the bullshit Trump routinely spewed—and reasoning that bulls cannot grab pussies because they lack hands (small hands or otherwise)—they turned the recovering Trump into a bull. They resolved that, the next time they delivered milk to Earth, they would reincarnate Philip Roth and invite him to serve as a writer-in-residence on Mammary.

(Pyg)malionized Trump Endures Regime Change

Professor Sondra Lear channeled her outrage in regard to Trump by watching Stephen Colbert and John Oliver decimate him. Sondra loved seeing the comedians describe how they both purchased wax figure presidents from a defunct Gettysburg wax museum. Statues of John Tyler and William Henry Harrison were rolled out on *The Late Show with Stephen Colbert.* Sondra laughed out loud when the statues where pushed together to imitate a kiss.

As Colbert turned to show a clip of Trump's outrage of the day, Sondra imagined transforming the president into a wax figure pig. "Pig, pig, pig," she shouted at Trump's televised image. English professor that she was, Sondra stopped shouting and thought of "Pygmalion." She resolved that somehow—even though she was not sure how—she would use a wax representation of Trump to do him in.

So she asked her friend Myra, a renowned feminist sculptor, to make a wax Trump figure. When Sondra saw the result, she sent Myra back to the drawing board.

"The depiction isn't right," said Sondra to her famous friend. "Trump has gotten a lot fatter since he took office. Please put more wax around his gut. And his mouth needs to be smaller."

Myra made the requested changes and wheeled the finished product into Sondra's apartment. Sondra stared at her wax figure Trump dead on.

"This is a Manhattan apartment. I don't have room for you," Sondra said to the statue. "I wish that I were Pygmalion and that I could make you real."

A feminist extraterrestrial materialized. "I'm Fyra," the alien said. "I've read all your feminist science fiction scholarly articles and I like them a lot. Your wish is my command. You desire to make your wax figure Trump real? Okay." Fyra snapped her fingers. "Wax Trump is now able to speak and walk. You can control what he says and where he goes. I can zap the three of us over to the White House. People will only be able to see wax Trump, not you and me. Are you in?"

"Sure."

Animate wax Trump and the now invisible Sondra and Fyra appeared in the Oval Office. Fyra beamed real Trump up to her spaceship. "Real Trump will be spending the rest of his life on a feminist separatist planet," Fyra stated to Sondra.

Wax Trump faced a phalanx of television cameras. "Think hard about what you want him to say," said Fyra. "Your thoughts will emanate from his tiny mouth."

"I resign from the office of president of the United States effective immediately," said wax Trump. Sondra had practiced what she preached to her Freshman English students about getting to the point.

"It's great to be rid of Trump. But we have a problem," said Sondra to Fyra.

"Which is?"

"Pence is the president."

"Not to worry."

When Pence took the oath of office, Sondra was very worried indeed. Fyra responded to Sondra's ashen face by explaining the situation further.

"You are not seeing real Pence. Real Pence joined real Trump in my spaceship. An alternative truth wax figure Pence took the oath. He functions just like wax Trump. You can control him. Go to it Sondra."

Sondra thought hard again. Wax Pence opened his mouth and uttered Sondra's words. "My fellow Americans," he said. "I have had a change of heart. I have metamorphosed—now there's a word that Trump would never say—from a conservative Christian to a liberal Democrat. I now see eye to eye with Elizabeth Warren, Chuck Schumer, and Nancy Pelosi. Hillary Clinton won the popular vote. Hillary is the rightful president of the United States. I will appoint Hillary as my vice president and resign to enable Hillary to replace me."

Sondra and Fyra smiled when they—while still invisible—saw Hillary take the oath of office. President Hillary Rodham Clinton and her vice president, Barack Obama, no alternative fact animated wax statues, were the real thing.

Sondra bid Fyra adieu and returned to academic business as usual. She was relieved that wax Trump was no longer taking up room in her apartment. While enjoying her reclaimed living space, she walked into the bedroom. "Hello Sondra," said wax John Tyler and wax William Henry Harrison as, on their own accord, they turned toward each other and began to kiss.

Marleen S. Barr

The Sheets Encounter Sheet Cake

or
Civic Virtue Triumphant Over Unrighteousness

The city . . . managed to get rid of only one statue in modern history - [']Civic Virtue['], a fountain depicting a large naked man standing (virtue) astride vanquished female figures representing vice and corruption. . . . Future generations are never going to see a bronze version of Trump astride his mount. Besides the detail of being perhaps the worst occupant of the White House in American history, our president doesn't ride. - Gail Collins, "Discovering the Limitations of Statues," *New York Times,* August 19, 2017, A21

The rightful place for 'Civic Virtue' is back at City Hall. - William K. Kregler [*a failed Republican candidate for Queens borough president*], "'Civic Virtue' Should Be Returned to City Hall," *Queens Ledger,* September 12, 2017

Part One:
Charlottesville and Washington, D.C.

It started as a prank. A Charlottesville denizen put eclipse glasses on the town's statue of General Robert E. Lee astride a horse. The prankster intended to announce that it was time to eclipse memorials to the Sons of Confederate Veterans. No one noticed when Lee's trusty horse blinked an eye. Not so when he bucked and Lee toppled down before running after his horse in hot pursuit.

Charlottesville's mayor, Michael Signer, was in charge of handling the Lee statue coming to life situation. The police, who were told to round up the horse and Lee, lassoed the former and locked the latter in a Monticello bedroom.

"I have been stuck standing in one place for years with Lee's ass on my back," the horse explained. "I want to run in a field with other horses. Give me a break."

Mayor Signer, deciding that the horse's request was reasonable, arranged for him to live in Blacksburg at the Virginia Tech Equine Center. Coping with Lee was another matter. Left to his own devices, Lee could wreak history altering havoc. Mayor Signer imagined him starting Civil War Two. Or, even worse, Trump, who loves generals, might make Lee a part of his administration.

When neo-Nazis and KKK members heard that Lee was incarcerated in Monticello, they descended on Charlottesville to liberate him. The Nazis carried lit tiki torches through the streets while shouting "Jews will not replace Lee." Sheet wearing KKK members stood outside Monticello and chanted "unlock Lee up, unlock Lee up."

Americans who disagreed with Nazis, KKK members, and Trump were heartsick. They related well to the solution Tina Fey enacted on *Saturday Night Live*. While stuffing her face with sheet cake, she explained that indulging in a sheet cake food orgy was a viable way to respond to Nazis marching in America. The multitudes of liberal women who now routinely drowned out their political sorrows by burying their heads in Häagen-Dazs quarts "got" Fey. With sheet cakes in hand, female liberal hordes amassed outside Monticello and confronted the KKK. They threw their sheet cakes at the sheets and successfully covered the white costumes' eye slits with frosting. Since visibility is an essential component of rampaging, the sheet cake nullified the sheets.

Trump weighed in on the Charlottesville situation. More specifically, Trump weighed more. Watching the sheet/sheet cake confrontation footage made him hungry. He ate an entire chocolate sheet cake covered with two scoops of vanilla ice cream. Liberals gagged when Trump stated that good people had come to Charlottesville with the intention of rescuing Lee. "Where does it stop?" Trump asked. "If a George Washington statue comes alive, are ya gonna lock up George in Mount Vernon?"

Mayor Signer, who had written a book on James Madison and, hence, was comfortable with American early national figures, entered Monticello to speak to Lee. "Hello General Lee," Signer said nonchalantly. "I decided to stop by on my way to synagogue. I'm Michael Signer, the mayor of Charlottesville. Nice to meet you."

"Are y'all tellin' me that the mayor of this here cotton pickin' little old town is a Jew? Do I hear a New York accent?" asked Lee.

"I grew up in northern Virginia and I received my B.A. at Princeton."

"Northern Virginia is north. New Jersey is really north. You, Mr. Mayor, are a damn Yankee Jew—and that's the worst kind."

Lee, shocked after learning that Charlottesville's mayor was Jewish, huffed and puffed and turned back into a statue. His transformation unleashed a force which caused all of America's Civil War memorial statues to come to life. Multitudinous formerly metallic iterations of Lee, Stonewall Jackson, P.G.T. Beauregard, Ambrose Burnside, and Jubal Early converged in Washington and gathered on the White House lawn. When Trump looked out of an Oval Office window and saw them, he responded by tweeting: "Too bad. All the come to life memorialized Civil War generals are guys. Can't rate 'em according to their looks. Can't grab their pussies. Sad."

Since all eyes were on the White House, no one noticed when the Lincoln Memorial's seated figure moved his foot. Lincoln rose from his chair, stretched, and walked down his memorial's stairs. He ended up joining the White House lawn gathering. Trump met Lincoln with an extended hand.

"There were more people at my inauguration than at your inauguration," Trump stated. "You did not have to deal with Crooked Hillary. Mar-a-Lago is more expensive real estate than your log cabin."

"Fourscore and seven years ago our fathers brought forth on this continent a new nation, conceived in liberty and dedicated to the proposition that all men are created equal," said Lincoln.

"I agree with ya when ya only mention men being created equal. But my father, who was a lot richer than your father—I had a huge father—brought forth in Queens's middle class housing which was dedicated to the proposition that black people should be prevented from living there. I'm dedicated to the proposition that Queens's real estate is not created equal to Manhattan's real estate."

"Now we are engaged in a great civil war," continued Lincoln as the Washington Monument detached itself from its foundation and floated over the White House. The monument acted as a bludgeon which made short shrift of the living former Civil War memorial statues. The statues turned back into metal upon impact. The metal heads, torsos, limbs, rifles, and horses which now littered the White House lawn were sent to recycling plants. Glad to see that America was finally free of Civil War monuments, Lincoln walked back to his memorial and sat down in his chair.

The Washington Monument, feeling happy that it had accomplished its mission, floated back to its foundation and reattached itself. Trump walked into the White House and buried his face in chocolate sheet cake.

Part Two:
Kew Gardens, Queens

Generations of Signer family members were proud of Mayor Michael Signer's contribution to American history. Skye Signer, his early twenty-second century descendant, was elected borough president of Queens. Skye, after growing up hearing how Mayor Signer dealt with the Lee statue, decided to tackle the abominable statue called "Civic Virtue Triumphant Over Unrighteousness" which was ugly and sexist to the extent that it had to be moved several times. It journeyed from outside City Hall to outside Queens Borough Hall in Kew Gardens to Green-Wood Cemetery. The cemetery was not its final resting place, though. In the wake of the misogyny the Trump administration unleashed, "Civic Virtue" was moved back to Kew Gardens immediately after Trump left office. It has remained there for more than a century.

Eons ago none other than sex texter Congressman Anthony Weiner took a break from posting images of his penis on the Internet to argue that "Civic Virtue" did not belong in Queens. Could he have been offended by a male sword-carrying nude stomping upon two writhing female figures with female heads and serpent tails named for the Sirens representing "vice" and "corruption?" Be that as it may, Weiner would have been better off posting the statue's crotch rather than his penis.

Skye agreed with Weiner. She decreed that "Civic Virtue" should be replaced by a statue of the most famous son of Queens, President Donald J. Trump. After "Civic Virtue" was demolished, Skye commissioned a statue which portrayed Trump riding in a golf cart. The fact that Mayor Fiorello H. La Guardia hated "Civic Virtue" to the extent that he called it "Fat Boy" inspired her decision. At the end of his days, Trump was a dead ringer for Henry the Eighth; unlike General Lee, Trump was too fat to sit on a horse—German draft horses included.

According to Skye's instructions, the Trump statue's small hands held a large dumpster. Queens's residents were asked to recycle their unwanted flying car batteries by depositing them in the dumpster. Skye authored the words set in stone above the Trump statue: "TRUMP LACKED CIVIC VIRTUE." The Trump statue erection site near the juncture of Queens Boulevard and Union Turnpike—a few blocks away from the Kew-Forest School Trump attended—was certainly appropriate. Young Trump could not have missed seeing "Civic Virtue" while on his way to elementary school.

Perhaps his teachers familiarized him with the words the sculptor Frederick William MacMonnies used to defend his statue. MacMonnies said, "What do I care if all the ignoramuses and quack politicians in New York, together with all the damn-fool women get together and talk about my statue? Let 'em cackle. Let 'em babble. You can't change the eternal verities that way. Can it be, that the women are angry because some man finally found the strength to resist temptation? . . . I think women should be pleased when strength is found to withstand their wonderful wiles" ["Civic Virtue," *Wikipedia*, https://en.wikipedia.org/wiki/Civic-Virtue]. Skye noted that MacMonnies' rant resounded as a precursor to Trump's tweet storms and misogynistic invective.

Charlottesville's Mayor Michael Signer memorial statue smiled when Skye's Trump statue was unveiled. In the manner of worshippers placing oranges as offerings in front of Buddha statues, people left sheet cakes in front of the Mayor Signer statue.

Despite Skye's good intention to erect a monumental insult to Trump, the Trump statue was a failure. Even in the twenty-second century, liberal New Yorkers still could not abide Trump. They hated the Trump statue as much as Mayor La Guardia hated "Civic Virtue." It was still almost impossible to remove offensive New York City statues. With Mayor Signer in mind, Skye solved the problem by covering the Trump statue with a huge sheet.

Donald and the Beanstalk

Melania strode across the White House lawn on her way to acquaint children from the Boys & Girls Clubs of Greater Washington with Michelle Obama's garden. While wearing her signature oversized sunglasses, she tried to dress appropriately for getting down to soil business. Her red plaid round white buttoned one thousand three hundred and eighty dollar Balmain designer shirt, matching red gardening gloves, black denim pants, and navy blue Converse sneakers were not garden variety gardening clothes. Balmain is a French luxury fashion line closely associated with the Kardashians.

She sat down in front of a huge tomato plant and began to speak to the children. "Thank you for coming and helping me to harvest and plant the vegetables in the beautiful garden. So I think we will have a lot of fun. So who has a garden at home?" Melania pointed at a girl named Tarshia's raised hand.

"I don't have a garden at home. I live in a homeless shelter," Tarshia said calmly. "You aren't Michelle. I miss Michelle. I don't like you. My brother says that you're nothing but a ho."

When Melania responded by leaning back against the plant, a large green tomato fell on her head. She went on as if nothing happened while speaking in the manner of a prostitute addressing a potential client. "Do you wanna go and have some fun?" she asked the children. "So when you leave today I wanna send you home with garden kits so you could continue gardening at home as well as honey from the White House hives so you can enjoy with your family and I hope you like it" ["First Lady Melania Trump White House Kitchen Garden Event September 22, 2017," *YouTube*, https://www.youtube.com/watch?v+YFbILYFOewQ].

Tarshia spoke without raising her hand. "I told you that I don't have a home. And honey—I can't give no honey to my family because my mom has diabetes. Honey could kill her."

"New York is where I'd rather stay. I get allergic smelling hay. I just enjoy a penthouse view," said Melania under her breath. She raised her voice and continued to speak in a prostitute-like manner: "Wanna come with me and have some fun? Let's put the gloves on. I brought mine too" ["First Lady Melania Trump White House Kitchen Garden Event September 22, 2017," *YouTube*, https://www.youtube.com/watch?v+YFbILYFOewQ].

She donned her gloves and picked up a large basket while knowing full well that the Trump administration had taken the gloves off vis-à-vis children's nutrition. The administration is supposedly making students' meals great again by allowing schools to request an exemption from the Obama era whole grain requirements and by again allowing students to drink one percent fat milk instead of skim milk. Casting this truth aside, Melania led the children into the garden. Tarshia picked up a trowel and started to dig. Her efforts were interrupted by a weird sound.

"I hear someone saying ho ho ho," Tarshia informed Melania. "It's not Christmas. Why is Santa Claus talking in your skanky assed garden?"

A tall greened skinned figure wearing a green mid-thigh length outfit emerged from behind a huge plant. "Good things from the garden, ho ho ho," the green individual said.

"Oh wow. A green person. You must be discriminated against big time," said Tarshia.

"I'm not a person. I'm the Jolly Green Giantess. Ho ho ho, Green Giantess."

"There must be some mistake," said Melania. "I have lived in America long enough to know that there is a male Jolly Green Giant, not a Jolly Green Giantess."

"Surprise," said the giantess. "The first Jolly Green Giant logo, created in 1928, was neither green nor jolly. He was hunched, downcast, and white. The twenty-first century is ready for a Jolly Green Giantess. So here I am." The giantess gave Tarshia three bean seeds. "Plant these. They will yield an amazing plant."

"Yes, ma'am," said Tarshia as she sowed the seeds.

The White House lawn rumbled as a huge beanstalk erupted and made its way toward the sky. Before anyone could stop her, Tarshia climbed to the beanstalk top. Upon arrival, she saw a room replete with gold furnishings. She stepped inside and was greeted by three figures. They looked like Trump—with some differences. All three had pink skin, snouts, and floppy ears. Their pink heads were covered with weird orange hair. They resembled the imagined progeny resulting after Trump's mother mated with a pig instead of with the orangutan Bill Maher famously described.

"Who are you?" Tarshia asked.

"We are the three little Trump pigs," the first Trump pig answered. I'm Frump and I represent how Trump looks in his oversized suits.

"I'm Chump," said the second Trump pig. I stand for the people who voted for Trump with the hope of bettering their lives."

"And I'm Dump," said the third Trump pig. "I portend what will happen to Trump when he is impeached."

"I don't want to stay in here with no Trump pigs. I want Michelle back," shouted Tarshia as she ran out of the room and slid down the beanstalk. When she landed back in the White House garden with a thud, she saw President Trump running toward the garden brandishing a hatchet.

"George Washington chopped down a cherry tree. Well I'm gonna go one better. I can't have something that is huger than me so near to the White House. It is enough that my whatever is dwarfed by the Washington Monument," said Trump as he began to hack at the beanstalk base.

The Jolly Green Giantess walked toward Trump.

"Now I have to contend with another minority group? The green people are rapists," said Trump. "We need to build a beautiful wall to keep the green people from comin' in. I will declare a green people travel ban."

"I don't think so," said the Jolly Green Giantess as she

grabbed Trump's hatchet out of his small hand. "I am bigger and stronger than you. If you ever do anything piggish again, I will huff and puff and blow your White House down."

"Melania, get your pants wearing ass back inside the White House pronto," ordered Trump. "You've planted enough for one day," said Trump as he followed her inside. Melania threw the Balmain shirt in the back of her closet. She never wore it again. She donated the red gloves to women who, due to Trump's policies, were beginning to resemble protagonists in *The Handmaid's Tale* and saved the Converse sneakers for the next hurricane photo op.

The Jolly Green Giantess became Tarshia's mentor. The girl grew and thrived to the extent that she went on to take a leading role in America's Green Party. The Green Party nominated Tarshia for president. Tarshia won. Resolved to undo all the damage Trump caused, Tarshia invited Michelle Obama to serve as Secretary of Agriculture. Secretary Obama made school food great. She made America great again too.

What Happened

or
'On What Planet Are You Living On?'

*I'm starting to enjoy Donald Trump's presidency. I
enjoy the rage it inspires in Laura Ingraham. On
news that the president had struck a tentative deal
with Democrats to help the beneficiaries of the
Deferred Action for Childhood Arrivals (DACA)
program in exchange for zero funding for his border
wall, the radio host and Trump groupie fumed, 'On
what planet are you living on?'* - Bret Stephens,
"Trump Gives Conservatives A Humbling," *New
York Times*, September 16, 2017, A19

The planet Triglyceride's Head Maternal Council was
scrupulously scanning the galaxy on the lookout for
patriarchal incursions against female humanoids. Council
member Kendra backed away from her console and cried out
in horror. "Look at this sexist atrocity," she screamed to her
colleagues. "I'm showing Code Orange."

"Code Orange?" questioned Kendra's supervisor Kara.
"The council has not seen Code Orange in eons. What's with
the Code Orange?"

"It's emanating from Earth. More specifically, the
signal comes from a new Earth leader's head. Looks like the
name's Dump or Clump or Grump. Oh, I see. It's Trump. His
head is over the top outrageous orange and his sexism is
egregious to the extent that he registers as Code Orange. I
can't believe it. He's broadcasting an image of a golf ball,"
explained Kendra.

"There's nothing wrong with golf balls. An Earth

astronaut mimicked hitting one on the moon," stated Kara.

"The golf ball is aimed at a woman's behind. It is causing her to fall forward."

"You are describing a Code Orange violent action perpetrated against a woman. This outrage calls for immediate intervention," the supervisor said.

"She is the most politically experienced woman in Earth country America's history."

"Are you referring to Hillary? The council loves Hillary. Hillary's involvement means we are facing Code Super Orange, a level we have never before reached. This is beyond the council's purview. This is a job for the Maternal Big Giant Head."

The M.B.G.H. materialized in the council chamber. "I know exactly how to stop Trump," she announced. "He comes from a long line of rapacious male entrepreneurs—with one exception. His paternal uncle, John George Trump, devoted himself to the life of the mind. John was an electrical engineering professor at M.I.T. who developed rotational radiation therapy and, with Robert J. Van de Graaf, created one of the first million-volt-x-ray generators."

"Sounds like death rays," said Kendra.

"Certainly does. But he used his expertise for cancer research and waste water treatment," the M.B.G.H. stated.

"He was a good guy."

"That's the point. We need to make it possible for Donald to be raised by his intellectual uncle John, not his mercantile father Fred. Fred first came to the council's attention during Earth year measurement circa 1927. We noticed that he attended Ku Klux Klan rallies and discriminated against black tenants. We didn't take action against Fred, though. In contrast, Donald becoming president constitutes a dire emergency. We have to initiate our most powerful Super Code Orange intervention mechanism."

"Are you referring to the Great Fertilized Egg Switcheroo?" Kendra asked.

"Exactly."

"Oh goody. I love the Switcheroo." It's so much fun to

remove a fertilized humanoid egg, zap it to Triglyceride for processing, and implant it in a host womb. Let's get the Switcheroo show on the road."

Kendra, Kara, and the M.B.G.H., who were invisible to the human eye, beamed down to 85-15 Wareham Road, Jamaica Estates, Queens, New York, America, Earth and entered the house's master bedroom at the exact moment when Fred Trump's sperm penetrated Mary Anne Trump's egg. They waved their hands over Mary Anne's abdomen. The two cells which would eventually become Donald Trump left Mary Anne's body and entered a test tube. The extraterrestrials transported the tube and themselves back to Triglyceride.

Immediately after reconvening in the council chamber, they chanted at the tube. "You will be composed of sugar, and spice, and everything nice," they said in unison.

"Time to return to Earth to transplant Donald in his host mother," stated Kara. The Triglycerideians transported themselves to Cambridge, Massachusetts and materialized in the bedroom John Trump shared with his wife, the former Flora Gordon Sauerbrun. They placed the two celled Donald within Flora's womb.

Flora gave birth to Donald Trump nine months later. Donald, who had no idea that John was not his biological father, emulated the elder Trump's devotion to scholarship. He watched John generate research and accompanied him to academic conferences. Donald was devoted to John to the extent that his "uncle" Fred's crass materialism disgusted him. In order to make his "father" proud, Donald pursued a Ph.D. in English at the University of Pennsylvania. Since Donald was made of sugar, and spice, and everything nice, he eventually became the head of the women's studies department at the Metropolitan University of New York. At Donald's request, "uncle" Fred built a huge black glass dormitory tower located at Fifth Avenue and Fifty-Ninth Street.

Professor Donald Trump was dedicated to feminist theory and women's studies pedagogy to the extent that he remained single until late in life. When Ruth Bader

Ginsburg's husband passed away, Donald professed his love for her. "I am very attracted to older women. You have a great legal mind. I rate your mind a ten. I love your mind. I love you. Marry me. If anyone grabs your pussy, I will defend you," Donald said to Ginsburg.

Ginsburg fell for the kindly women's studies professor. After Donald converted to Judaism, they got married at Temple Emanu-El located a few blocks north of the Trump MUNY Dormitory Tower. Several Triglycerideians attended the wedding and the reception held in the Tower lobby. The reception's highlight occurred when Donald went down the escalator followed by Ginsburg to announce their support for the MUNY Human Diversity Initiative.

Two years later, the Triglycerideians returned to Earth to witness the inauguration of America's first Jewish female President.

"I swear to preserve, protect, and defend the Constitution of the United States of America," said the at that moment sworn in president of the United States of America Ruth Bader Ginsburg. Donald, America's first first gentleman, beamed with pride as he stood beside his wife. "Your Inauguration Day crowd is huge. It is bigger than Obama's crowd," Donald said to her. He was telling the truth.

"I'm so glad that we did the Switcheroo. Bringing the Trump embryo to Triglyceride and chanting really worked," said Kendra to the M.B.G.H.

"Under President Ginsburg, American women never had it so good. They think that *The Handmaid's Tale* is fiction, not impending reality," the M.B.G.H. stated. "Vice President Hillary Clinton just released *What Happened* to explain how it came to pass that two amazing women are now running America. Of course she will never know what *really* happened.

Trump In Limbo

After Trump spent days fighting with Myeshia Johnson, the widow of fallen American soldier La David Johnson, CNN anchor Don Lemon wrote a scathing letter to Trump and read it on the air. He then spoke with political commentator Ana Navarro who wondered how low Trump could go.

Suddenly Lemon and Navarro found themselves standing in the Oval Office holding the ends of a long pole. Trump walked in and glared at them. Navarro, even though she had lost control of her location, continued what she was saying to Lemon. "Just how low can you go?" she shouted at Trump.

"Are you challenging me?" Trump questioned. "And as for you Don Lemon, you're a light weight fake news purveyor. I'm a Don too. My Don is bigger than your Don. I will not respond to your letter."

"I repeat, how low can you go?" questioned Navarro while she and Lemon continued to hold the poll.

"I'll show you," said Trump as he shimmied under it. "I'm doin' the Limbo. It's an Hispanic thing popular during my youth. You're Hispanic, Ana. You should get what I'm doin'."

"I don't understand how a big fat pig like you can fit under this low pole. It makes as little sense as my being here," responded Navarro.

A sign which said "magic realism, it's an Hispanic thing" appeared hanging from the pole. Trump emerged from under the pole in the guise of a pig. When Lemon and Navarro again lowered the pole, Pig Trump still made it under. Then they moved the pole to the extent that it was five inches above the floor.

"You think that I can't go as low as that. Well think again," said Pig Trump as he turned into a rat. "Rats can go through holes the size of a quarter" said Rat Trump as he scurried under the pole. The sight of Rat Trump caused Lemon and Navarro to shriek and drop the pole.

"I can go low enough to fit under a pole flush with the floor," said Rat Trump as he was undergoing another metamorphosis. He turned into a red circular entity. His arms and legs were attached to his new round core.

Melania walked into the Oval Office. "I regret to inform you that your husband had been transformed into a pig and a rat. He is now a red circle with white gloved and white shoed appendages," intoned Lemon in his most matter of fact news anchor voice.

"The circle has an 'm' on it," Melania stated. "The 'm' must stand for 'Melania.' Donald is trying to communicate with me."

Circular Trump ran back and forth under and around the pole. "I won. I won the how low can you go Limbo contest," announced Circular Trump. "The 'm' has nothing to do with you, Melania. I've turned into a beautiful red M&M's candy. Russian red is the most important color in my life. I've become a red M&M's to fit under the pole—and to signal to Vlad that I am ready to cut another huge sweet deal with him."

"You have a big lying mouth and small pussy grabbing hands—which are now smaller than they were before. But, even though you are now M&M's Trump, melting in people's mouths and not in their hands is too good for you," shouted Navarro as she poured a glass of water over M&M's Trump. M&M's Trump melted. He became a red stain which merged with the floor. "Now we can finally see exactly how low Trump can go."

A bag of Reese's Pieces appeared on the Oval Office desk. The sign attached to it said "Eat me."

"I think that we should do what the sign says," said Lemon.

"Good decision," said the ghost of Gabriel Garcia Márquez who was floating below the Oval Office ceiling. He pointed at the pole. It turned into a snake. An apple appeared next to the snake. The apple had a sign taped to it which also said "Eat me."

Melania picked up the apple.

"CNN is running an ad about facts which states that an apple is not a banana," said Lemon. "Perhaps this apple represents the truth CNN advocates. Eat the apple, Melania."

She took a bite. She was thrown out of the Rose Garden, which became the snake's new home, forever. Márquez dematerialized. Immediately after eating some Reese's Pieces, Lemon and Navarro found themselves back in the CNN studio.

"Ladies and gentleman,' said Lemon as he solemnly looked into the camera. "Trump has besmirched the Presidency. Donald J. Trump will forever be in limbo. That is a real fact."

"Trump will never lower our country again," added Navarro.

Carmen Miranda's ghost appeared on the set. The camera focused on the apples and bananas which adorned her headpiece. "Miranda's use of fruit is a much more creative and healthy approach to Hispanic culture than Trump's obsession with taco bowls," said Navarro. Anderson Cooper described the occurrence on "The Ridiculist" portion of his program.

A sign appeared on the red stained Oval Office floor. "I apologize to Myeshia Johnson," it said.

Trump's New Reality TV Gig: 'Survivor, Puerto Rico'

The New York subway system's garbage train best describes the spaceship which hovered over the White House. The Metropolitan Transportation Authority refuse rig, akin to a freight train, slowly collects ninety tons of track garbage per day. The spaceship, built by denizens of the feminist separatist planet Gonad to remove intergalactic debris, is as plodding and odiferous as the garbage train. After designating Trump as a menace to female Earthlings, the Gonadians sent a garbage spaceship to Earth to dispose of him.

When Trump walked across the White House lawn, he looked up and noticed a large vacuum cleaner hose dangling in the sky. The hovering hose sucked him in. Once inside, he saw a taco bowl on a shelf. A sign in front of the bowl said "eat me." Trump scarfed the bowl down. His already fat ass instantaneously became huge to the extent that it got stuck in the hose. A sign which said "drink me" then appeared in front of a liquid filled glass. Since Trump does not imbibe alcohol, he was happy that the glass contained lemonade. After he drank the lemonade, his ass returned to its usual corpulence. Trump's upward trajectory continued until he landed with a thud inside the ship's hold. He was surrounded by broken satellites and meteorites. A woman wearing a red one piece bathing suit and thigh high sequined red boots appeared in the junk filled hold. The red and gold sash draped across her body read "Puerto Rico."

Trump, thinking that he was closely encountering a familiar situation, became emboldened. "Hello Miss Puerto Rico," he said. "Beauty pageant contestants routinely allow me to grab their pussies. You're beyond a ten."

"After extensively studying American Earth culture, I learned that 'pussy' often refers to the female humanoid body part relevant to reproduction and excretion. It is impossible for you to grab my pussy. I don't have one," said the Gonadian.

"A pussyless woman is useless," stated Trump. "Yeah, pussies become old and dry. When that happens with one of my wives, I dispose of her and get a new young pussy. A pussy like yours, for instance. How can you be pussyless?"

"I am Karmen. I come in peace from the feminist separatist planet Gonad. Gonadians are devoid of vaginas. Our reproductive and biological functions are beyond your purview. For your purposes, Gonadians have a whatever. If I were you, I would not try to grab my whatever."

"I can't believe that Hugh Heffner is dead and I have been sucked up by a Playboy Bunny lookalike who claims to be a feminist pussyless space alien."

"That is correct."

"What the hell am I doin' in here?"

"You are human garbage. My job is to dispose of you. Your fellow humanoid Lin-Manuel Miranda authored this tweet: 'You're going straight to hell, @realDonaldTrump. No long lines for you. Someone will say, 'Right this way, sir.' They'll clear a path' [@Lin-Manuel, *Twitter*, 7:21 AM, September 30, 2017]. I am the path clearer. You're going straight to hell. Right this way, sir."

"I get it. I'm dead. Your red outfit means that you're the devil. Can I make a huge deal with you?" Trump's ability to make a Faustian deal was limited. Although he read *Doctor Faustus* in the English course he took during his stint as a Fordham undergraduate, his professor gave him a "C."

"Absolutely not. You are not dead. I am sending you to a hell on Earth which is partly of your own making."

Trump found himself back inside the vacuum cleaner hose. This time he was being sucked downward. He landed in a flooded house. The roof was torn off. The home's contents were water sodden and scattered. The interior stunk. Karmen walked toward Trump.

"Where am I?" Trump asked.

"Arecibo, Puerto Rico in the wake of Hurricane Maria.

You're on your own in survivor mode," said Karmen as she threw a roll of paper towels at Trump's head.

"What the hell do you think you're doin' puttin' me in Puerto Rico hell? I'm the president of the United States. I'm very rich. I'm a huge person. The Secret Service will save me."

"No one can see you. No one can hear you. You have a mouth. You can scream. You can do whatever you want. But your efforts won't do you any good. For the first time in your privileged life, you will have to scrounge to survive."

"I'll be fine. Puerto Ricans should be very proud that hundreds of people haven't died after Hurricane Maria as they did in a real catastrophe like Katrina. Every death is a horror. But, if you look at a real catastrophe like Katrina, and you look at the tremendous hundreds and hundreds and hundreds of people that died and you look at what happened here with really a storm that was just totally overpowering. . . . No one has ever seen anything like this and I hate to tell you, Puerto Rico, but you've thrown our budget a little out of whack because we've spent a lot of money on Puerto Rico. And that's fine, we've saved a lot of lives" [Juana Summers, "Trump Attacks San Juan Mayor Over Hurricane Response," http://www.cnn.com/2017/09/30/politics/trump-tweets-puerto-rico-mayor/index.html].

Karmen disappeared. Trump slept in the house on the dirt floor. In the morning, he found a broken bottle and went to a stream to fill it with potable water. He walked through Arecibo famished. The smell of food emanating from people communally cooking in the street made him even hungrier. At nightfall, he scavenged food from a garbage bag left near the flooded house. Removed from human community, Trump was an apprentice refugee who had been fired from life.

Trump made his way to a shelter and slid beneath an empty cot so that no one would step on his invisible self. He continued to scavenge food from garbage bags. Karmen reappeared just as Puerto Rico was beginning to restore its communications and electrical infrastructure. "You've suffered enough," she said. "You will now be able to be seen and heard again."

After Trump contacted the Secret Service, he was flown

back to Washington. Like Doctor Manette emerging from the Bastille, Trump was irrevocably changed. He could no longer cope with living in the White House or Trump Tower. He rented a modest apartment in Washington Heights and remained in the neighborhood for the rest of his life. With the "West Side Story" score incessantly blaring in the background, Trump happily ate authentic beans and rice instead of taco shell bowls

Despite his metamorphosis, Trump was still Trump. He dumped Melania and married a twenty-something neighborhood woman named Maria.

The Gonadians named his experience 'Survivor, Puerto Rico' and watched episodes on their telepathic mind screens. The show was a huge hit.

Trump Takes Stock of His Scarlet Letter As Big As the Ritz

The witches are coming, but not for your life. We're coming for your legacy. The cost of being Harvey Weinstein is not getting to be Harvey Weinstein anymore. We don't have the justice system on our side; we don't have institutional power; we don't have millions of dollars or the presidency; but we have our stories, and we're going to keep telling them. - Lindy West, "Yes, This Is a Witch Hunt," *New York Times,* October 18, 2017, A7

There's a pig in the White House. He was in Japan this week and they took him to a sushi place and they asked if he would like some yellow tail and he said 'sure, what's her name?' I mean he's a pig. He's a pig. - Bill Maher, *Real Time With Bill Maher,* HBO, November 10, 2017

Millions of American women dusted off their pussy hats before converging outside Harvey Weinstein's residence. While waving lit tiki torches and chanting "men will not replace us," they extricated Weinstein from his home, placed him in a huge box, and FedExed the box to the White House lawn. Upon the box's arrival, women unpacked Weinstein, ripped his clothes off, tarred and feathered him, and locked him up in a pillory.

Female battalions, in the manner of revolutionaries storming Versailles, stood outside the White House and demanded that Trump emerge from within immediately if not sooner. The Secret Service took no action when the women locked up Trump in stocks alongside Weinstein. Since Weinstein and Trump are far from thin, the women had to scrape the bottom of the tar and feather barrel to cover Trump.

The assembled women cheered at the sight of naked captured sexual predators positioned as a reality television public ridicule spectacle. They stopped cheering when a hearse pulled up. Enraged women opened two caskets, removed the corpses, and placed them in other sets of stocks. They had exhumed Hugh Hefner and Roger Ailes. Former undercover Playboy Bunny Gloria Steinem attached pig ears and a pig tail to Heffner's corpse. Gwyneth Paltrow, who had just finished accusing Weinstein of sexually harassing her early in her career, showed up and told Steinem that the pig accoutrements served Hefner right.

Jane Fonda approached Trump and Weinstein while they were frantically waving their confined hands. She eyed their naked bodies and told the crowd that "these big fat guys have really small penises."

"My penis is huge. I have a beautiful huge penis," Trump shouted. Fonda put masking tape over Trump and Weinstein's mouths as women grabbed the men's crotches.

Meryl Streep stepped forward to tie signs which said "prick" to their penises. For good measure, she attached a scarlet letter "G"—which stood for "grabber"—to the tar covering their chests.

All eyes turned to the sky as a witch flying on a broom appeared overhead. "The casting couch was operative when I played the Wicked Witch of the West in *The Wizard of Oz*," shouted Margaret Hamilton. The crowd saluted her as she disappeared over the horizon.

Melania, dressed like a *Les Misérables* extra, walked out of the White House carrying a ladle and a pail filled with soup made from Purina Pig Chow. She spooned the soup into Trump and Weinstein's gaping mouths.

In retribution for all the women whose lives had been ruined by male serial predators, it was determined that Trump and Weinstein would spend the rest of their days publicly taking stock of themselves while being locked up in stocks. They became Washington's biggest tourist attraction. Hefner and Ailes were re-interned when their remains began to stink as much as their degradation of women.

Women, empowered by #MeToo, insisted that sexist pigs who routinely sexually assault women would no longer be tolerated—and should not serve as the president of the United States. They turned their attention to inaugurating the rightful president.

Hillary Rodham took the oath of office before a crowd which was huger than the paltry audience for Trump's inauguration. There was no second President Clinton. President Hillary Rodham, fed up with her husband's sexual transgressions, divorced him.

Hillary spent the first months of her administration tirelessly working to reverse Trump's efforts to undo everything President Obama had accomplished. When taking a well-deserved rest, she looked up from her Oval Office desk and saw an extravagantly attired woman wearing a diamond as big as the Ritz coming toward her.

"Hello Ivana, what can I do for you?" asked Hillary.

"I felt sorry for Donald having to eat pig slop every day. So I came to feed him a taco bowl shell," said Ivana Trump in her Czech accent. "Melania deserved to become a pig food dispenser. I am the rightful first lady. I want to be the first lady. Sure we have nothing in common. But opposites attract. Hillary, will you marry me?"

Conservatives' heads exploded when Hillary and Ivana got married in the White House. Hillary wore a gold pantsuit and her own diamond as big as the Ritz. Ivana stepped outside and shoved some wedding cake into Trump and Weinstein's mouths. When Margaret Hamilton made a return broom flight to the White House, she wrote "the pigs have surrendered" in the sky.

Marleen S. Barr

Trumpzilla the Humongous Missile Monster Fires the Little Rocket Man

Is there no one that Donald Trump doesn't make look better? - Gail Collins, "Sex, Senators and - Oh Gosh, Mitt," *New York Times,* November 11, 2017, A20

Upon arrival in Japan, Trump addressed American troops who gave him a bomber jacket. As the president was zipping his jacket, Kim Jong-un launched a missile directly over Trump's head causing him to inhale its fumes.

Trump's chest suddenly expanded to the extent that the zipper burst open. As Trump became huger and huger, a long tail popped out from behind his behind. "My penis is bigger than this new-fangled tail," said Trump while impressed with his second bodily protuberance. The metamorphosis was complete when Trump, now looking as monstrous as he was in fact, became an orange fur covered incredible hulk resembling a cross between a Wookie and a long tailed King Kong.

Trumpzilla, as the president was now called, truly became the unimaginable antithesis of the elegant and cool Obama. Melania was reduced to enacting "Beauty and the Beast" on steroids. Well used to accompanying a boorish lumbering clod, she soldiered on at Trumpzilla's side as he crashed into a reception Prime Minister Shinzō Abe arranged.

Despite his enormous change at the last minute, Trumpzilla was still the president of the United States. He was no more easily removed from office than the original President Trump. Trumpzilla was the only sentient entity who made Donald Trump look better. Trumpzilla was horrifying to the extent that liberals who now thought that George W. Bush and Mitt Romney were tolerable in relation to Trump, were becoming nostalgic for the original Donald Trump. The original merely had a big mouth and a big ass.

Unable to fit inside Air Force One, Trumpzilla adhered to his Asia trip itinerary by swimming to South Korea. He smashed the desks in the South Korean National Assembly chamber and began to address the body: "Kim Jong-un's worst human rights violation is that his rocket fumes changed me into Trumpzilla. This is more horrible than all the North Koreans he starved and tortured. I am the most important thing on Earth," Trumpzilla screamed as he thumped his tail for emphasis. "But let me talk about something positive. Golf for instance. South Koreans have made huge strides in golf. A South Korean won the tournament held at my golf course in Bedminster, New Jersey. Did ya hear that world? I'm usin' my position as president of the United States to promote my golf course. This self-promotion is much more important than the potential of nuclear war that could incinerate a million people. Come to think of it, Seoul, located right smack in the middle of the Korean Peninsula, is a great location for a beautiful Trump golf course. Bring on the nuclear war to level Seoul so that I can develop the land to contain nothing other than Trump golf courses and Trump towers. I'll start the nuclear war myself in order to do this huge real estate deal."

Trumpzilla lumbered across the DMZ and headed straight for the North Korean missile launch facility. He entered the facility, found the launch control panel, timed blast off for ten minutes later, pushed the "send" button, ran to a missile silo, opened the hatch, and wrapped his arms around the missile he found within. "Short and fat little rocket man, meet the humongous missile monster. I'm firing your missile—and you're fired," Trumpzilla shrieked. "My penis and my tail are bigger than your missile," he bellowed as the missile rose with him and he held on to it in the manner of a twenty-first century Dr. Strangelove.

Luckily, Trumpzilla was as unqualified as his former self. He set the missile's launch codes incorrectly and, hence, caused its trajectory to be continuously straight up rather than ultimately perpendicular to the Earth. The missile and Trumpzilla crashed into the moon in the manner of Georges Méliès iconic "A Trip to the Moon" image of the bullet shaped space capsule gouging out the Man in the Moon's eye. South Korean President Moon Jae-in was relieved that a bombed and leveled Seoul did not become Trumpzilla's new real estate development site.

He was also relieved that Trumpzilla did not have the opportunity to meet with Kim Jong-un in, say, Singapore. The South Korean president imagined that during this meeting Trumpzilla, in an effort to establish a dynastic dictatorship of his own, would agree to rename himself Kim Don-jon and, to add to his coffers, proclaim that North Korea would become America's fifty-first state. It was beyond credence to embellish this ludicrous scenario by believing that Trumpzilla could possibly make the following statement: "They [North Koreans] have great beaches. You see that whenever they're exploding the cannons into the ocean. I said look at that view. Wouldn't that make a great condo beyond that?" [Nina Golgowski, "North Korea 'Could Have The Best Hotels' On Its Beaches, Trump Raves to Kim," *HuffPost*, June 12, 2018, https://www.huffingtonpost.com/entry/north-korea-best-hotels-beaches-trump-kim_us_5b1fc2a1e4b0bbb7a0e18c73]. Not even Trumpzilla would try to market North Korea as the new Boca and treat the threat of nuclear war as a real estate deal.

***

In the mid twenty-second century, to commemorate her ancestor Trumpzilla, Lunaka Trump built a golf course on the moon's North Korean missile landing site. The project was a huge failure. Yes, astronaut Alan Shepard simulated playing golf on the moon. Feminist extraterrestrials, who had turned the moon into a vacation destination and hence controlled its economy, unlike the suburban Americans Shepard represented, do not play golf.

Coda: 'So Many People to Attack, So Little Time'

or
Kim Jong-un Blasts Off

In his brief career as president and a candidate for president, Mr. Trump has attacked virtually every major institution in American life: Congress, the courts, Democrats, Republicans, the news media, the Justice Department, Hollywood, the military, NATO, the intelligence agencies, the cast of 'Hamilton,' the cast of 'Saturday Night Live,' the pope and now professional sports. . . . 'The Trump credo seems to be so many people to attack, so little time,' said Peter Wehner, a former strategic adviser to President George W. Bush and now a senior fellow at the Ethics and Public Policy Center. - Peter Baker, "Divider Not a Uniter, the President Widens the Breach," *New York Times,* September 25, 2017, A15

Trump attacked Kim Jong-un by calling him "the little rocket man."

It was evident that their fight was really about penis size, not ballistics. Kim Jong-un, wanting to show the world that his penis was bigger than the American dotard's, attached himself to a nuclear missile headed for the White House.

Trump exploded when he saw the missile and Kim Jung-un coming.

Kim Jong-un and the missile landed on the White House lawn.

Kaboom!

THE END

"I think that was the thrust of it." - Mel Brooks [Stephen Deusner, "Mel Brooks: 'The Only Weapon I've Got Is Comedy,'" *salon.com,* November 14, 2012, https://www.salon.com/2012/11/14/mel_brooks_the_only _weapon_ive_got_is_comedy/]

Marleen S. Barr is known for her pioneering work in feminist science fiction and teaches English at the City University of New York. She has won the Science Fiction Research Association Pilgrim Award for lifetime achievement in science fiction criticism. Barr is the author of *Alien to Femininity: Speculative Fiction and Feminist Theory*, *Lost in Space: Probing Feminist Science Fiction and Beyond*, *Feminist Fabulation: Space/Postmodern Fiction*, and *Genre Fission: A New Discourse Practice for Cultural Studies*. Barr has edited many anthologies and co-edited the science fiction issue of *PMLA*. Barr's novels, which like *When Trump Changed* feature protagonist Professor Sondra Lear, are *Oy Pioneer!* and *Oy Feminist Planets: A Fake Memoir*